D0361388

Today's Apostasy

How "Decisionism" Is Destroying Our Churches

Today's Apostasy: How "Decisionism" Is Destroying Our Churches
© 1999 by R. L. Hymers, Jr., and Christopher Cagan

All rights reserved. We encourage the use of this material; however, in order to protect the contents from change, neither this book, nor any part thereof, may be reprinted in any form without written permission from the publisher, except for brief excerpts used in magazine reviews, etc.

Printed in the United States of America

Published by:
Hearthstone Publishing, Ltd.
P.O. Box 815   Oklahoma City, OK 73101
405/789-3885   888/891-3300   FAX 405/789-6502

ISBN 1-57558-046-2

Today's Apostasy

How "Decisionism" Is Destroying Our Churches

R. L. Hymers, Jr.
Christopher Cagan

This book is dedicated to the memory of Dr. Hymers' mother,

Cecelia
(May 20, 1913–December 18, 1997)
She sat beside him and encouraged him as he worked on the final copy of this book. Her own conversion at the age of eighty was instrumental in motivating us to write it;

and to

Dr. Henry M. McGowan
who with his late wife, Joyce, took Dr. Hymers to a Baptist church when he was thirteen years old. Without their encouragement he would not be a pastor today.

Today's Apostasy: How "Decisionism" Is Destroying Our Churches

by R. L. Hymers, Jr., M.Div., D. Min., Th.D.
and Christopher Cagan, Ph.D., M.Div., Ph.D.

Many have noticed that the spiritual condition of this generation is comparable to the days of Noah, but few have understood how such apostasy came about. How did so many denominations become apostate in the last hundred years? Why do seventy-four percent of our people claim to be saved without this having a more positive effect on our crumbling society? Why do so many preachers commit immorality? Why do our churches seem unable to hold on to most of their young people? Why no major revival for over ninety years? This book gives an answer to those questions.

Foreword

Remember the days of old, consider the years of many generations. . . .
                                                —Deuteronomy 32:7

. . . Ask for the old paths, where is the good way, and walk therein,
and ye shall find rest for your souls.
                                                —Jeremiah 6:16

Dr. Hymers and Dr. Cagan have rediscovered some of the old
paths of evangelistic preaching and personal counselling; paths all
but given up in many of our churches.

My own involvement in this type of ministry started with a conversation. I introduced myself to Dr. Hymers at a preachers' get-
together we both attended. We began to discuss things biblical
and theological, as preachers usually do. At some point he asked
me, "You counsel all your church members yourself, don't you?" I
assured him that I did. He then said in his soft voice, "But you let
someone else deal with them about their salvation, don't you?"
That struck a chord in my heart. Nothing is more important than
getting saved. I started thinking.

Our nation is dying. Our way of life has almost disappeared
from the scene. Our culture has been wrenched from our grasp
and replaced by a cruel and hateful paganism. This has happened
because Christianity in America has become impotent. The problem began when preachers stopped listening to the sinners who

responded to their Gospel sermons. As a result of not listening to sinners who responded to the call of the Gospel, preachers gradually lost touch with those to whom they were preaching.

When people said they wanted to get saved, I discovered that I didn't know what they meant, or what they really believed, because I never asked them. Saved from what? I never knew. Saved by whom? I had not a clue concerning who they meant when they said, "Jesus," because there are so many false concepts of Christ today.

R. L. Hymers has a vigorous church in the civic center of Los Angeles because he has resorted to an old-fashioned practice employed by nearly every Gospel-preaching, Christ-exalting pastor in the English-speaking world before Charles G. Finney changed evangelism in the last century. Instead of shaking everyone's hand after church, Hymers actually listens to sinners. He stays behind in his office for an hour or so after every service to do this with a few trained counsellors. That's something every preacher used to do, but few do it today. Dr. Hymers listens to sinners.

The goal of this book is to get preachers and counsellors to listen. Why? Dr. Hymers and Dr. Cagan show the horrible results of not doing so. Not listening has produced hundreds of thousands of lost church members, including lost preachers. It is not at all uncommon these days to hear of pastor after pastor falling into adultery, and then resuming his pastorate at another church, too often with another wife! And it's really no different with church members. How many medium- to small-sized churches have a group of qualified deacons anymore? Many of our churches are dying because pastors are not taking time to listen and make sure the people are in Christ.

I watched Dr. Hymers doing personal work after he preached a few times. After he concluded, I questioned him. At times I challenged him. And I examined the results. For three years now I have been listening to sinners who respond to my Gospel sermons. This is spiritual obstetrics, bringing sinners into the new birth. This is wrestling for anxious souls. This is spiritual warfare. Oh, how I love this work! I never knew what being an undershepherd was before I began it. I knew what preaching was. I knew what counselling was. But being a shepherd?

Sheep have a very high mortality rate when lambing time comes on a sheep ranch, if the shepherd isn't right there to "pull" those lambs. It seems that God created sheep in such a way that they need shepherds to help the birthing process. Men of God, back in the days when life was more rural and agricultural, knew this and did this. Now I do this. When it's lambing time at my church, when I've concluded my message, I am right there "pulling" those lambs. I'm sitting with them, one by one, listening to sinners and pointing them to the Savior. I have found that it's worthwhile knowing what what those sinners think about subjects which determine whether they spend eternity in Heaven or Hell.

Read this book. It could be the most important thing you read this year, because it will make you think about effective evangelism.

—Rev. John S. Waldrip
Calvary Road Baptist Church
Monrovia California

The dark days that preceded the Great Awakening will come again unless somebody stands firmly and clearly and decidedly by the doctrine of a converted church membership.

—Rev. F. L. Chappell
"The Great Awakening of 1740" (written in 1903)

How did the scourge of modernism every succeed in wiping out the true Gospel from so many Western Protestant denominations over the last hundred years? And what caused countless evangelical churches to capsize before the tide of "worldly" Christianity which arose only three decades ago?

—Dr. Peter Masters
pastor of Spurgeon's Tabernacle (written in 1976)

And many false prophets shall rise, and shall deceive many. . . .

—Matthew 24:11

Examine yourselves, whether ye be in the faith. . . .

—2 Corinthians 13:5

Marvel not that I said unto thee, Ye must be born again.

—John 3:7

Chapter One

The Days of Noah

Between 3,500 and 4,000 churches close their doors each year in the USA.

—Dr. Woodrow Kroll
The Vanishing Ministry

We are a society poised on the brink of self-destruction. Our culture is plagued with crime and violence, drug abuse, racial and ethnic tension, broken families and corruption.

—Billy Graham, upon receiving the Congressional Gold Medal
from the U.S. Congress and President Clinton

. . . Tell us, when shall these things be? and what shall be the sign of thy coming, and of the end of the world?

—Matthew 24:3

The disciples asked for a sign that would show how close we are to the end of the world. On two separate occasions Christ had cautioned them against speculating about the exact time (Matthew 24:36; Acts 1:7). However, He did give them a number of signs that would indicate its approaching nearness: "And when these things begin to come to pass, then look up, and lift up your heads; for your redemption draweth nigh" (Luke 21:28).

Since all the signs are currently visible on the world stage, it appears that we are now moving rapidly toward the end of history, and to the close of this present age. Here are five of the most important signs:

- The reestablishment of Israel, with the Jews returning to their God-given homeland (Luke 21:24; Matthew 24:32–34; Ezekiel 37:21; 38:8).
- The rise of the "Common Market," a coalition of nations in Europe, moving toward union (Daniel 2:40–45; Revelation 17:12).
- The increase of worldwide persecution against Christians and Jews (Matthew 24:9–10; Jeremiah 30:7; Daniel 12:1).
- The increase of worldwide famines and imbalanced ecology (Matthew 24:7).
- The rise of apostasy in Christianity (2 Thessalonians 2:3; Matthew 24:11–12).

The greatest sign, however, is given in Matthew 24:37–39, where Jesus said:

> But as the days of Noe were, so shall also the coming of the Son of man be. For as in the days that were before the flood they were eating and drinking, marrying and giving in marriage, until the day that Noe entered into the ark, And knew not until the flood came, and took them all away; so shall also the coming of the Son of man be.

Dr. M. R. DeHaan, the late prophetic radio preacher, gave the following comments on those verses:

> Jesus says, if you want to know the signs of My coming, study the days of Noah before the flood. When the conditions which existed before the flood are repeated, then know that it is near. This leaves anyone who has a Bible without excuse. Everything we know about the days before the flood is recorded in three chapters of the Bible (Genesis 4, 5, and 6). These three chapters can be read in thirty minutes. . . . Since all we know about the days to which Jesus

refers as the days of Noah is found in the Bible, no one can plead ignorance. To understand Jesus' words concerning the sign of His return we need only to study the three chapters dealing with the subject (Genesis 4, 5, and 6).[1]

Since the purpose of this book is conversion, we will examine the days of Noah from that perspective. Genesis 4:26 tells us: "And to Seth, to him also there was born a son; and he called his name Enos: then began men to call upon the name of the LORD."

Enos died in the year 1140 after the Creation, eighty-four years after Noah was born (1,056 years after the creation). Since people lived between eight and nine hundred years, many thousands of people who "called on the name of the Lord" in Enos' day were still living in Noah's day. It should be remembered that there were only two lifetimes between the Creation and the Flood.

Dr. Henry M. Morris indicates that "Adam lived until Lamech, the father of Noah, was fifty-six years old, and Noah was born only fourteen years after the death of Seth."[2] This means that there were many people still living who had "called on the name of the Lord" when the Flood came. If each couple had an average of ten children, that would mean that there were about eight million people on earth at the time of the Flood.

They Called on the Name of the Lord, Yet Drowned in the Flood

Genesis 4:26 says, ". . . then **began** men to call upon the name of the LORD." The verse indicates that this "calling" continued for some time, which means that **a large number of those who drowned in the Flood had called on the Lord's name, but were not saved.** As God said later to the prophet Isaiah: ". . . This people draw near me with their mouth, and with their lips do honour me, but have removed their heart far from me . . ." (Isaiah 29:13).

This was the case in Noah's day as well. Keeping in mind the fact that uncounted multitudes had "called on the name of the Lord" in Noah's day, and yet were drowned, the words of Jesus take on deep meaning: "But as the days of Noe were, so shall also the coming of the Son of man be . . . [they] knew not until the flood came and took them all away" (Matthew 24:37, 39).

The people of Noah's day had "a form of godliness" (2 Timothy 3:5), but were destroyed in the waters of the Flood because they were unsaved:

> . . . For **all flesh** had corrupted his way upon the earth. And God said unto Noah, The end of **all flesh** is come before me; for the earth is filled with violence through them; and; behold, I will destroy them with the earth.
> —Genesis 6:12–13

Out of all the multiplied thousands who had called on the name of the Lord, only Noah and his family were saved. "And (God) spared not the old world, but saved Noah the eighth person, a preacher of righteousness, bringing in the flood upon the world of the ungodly" (2 Peter 2:5).

We conclude that those who called on the Lord, but were destroyed in the Flood, were unsaved people who went to Hell, since Peter calls them "the ungodly" in verse five, and gives them as an illustration of those who are reserved ". . . unto the day of judgment to be punished" (2 Peter 2:9).

Jesus said that these conditions would be repeated at the end of this age.

A Repetition in Our Time

Today, millions of people have called on the name of the Lord and think they are converted. But many are not. They have not come into the ark of salvation. They are not in Christ. They are religious, but lost.

God said of the people in Noah's day: ". . . My spirit shall not always strive with man . . ." (Genesis 6:3). The Hebrew word translated "strive" is *dîn*. It means "judge." Dr. H. C. Leupold pointed out that the Holy Spirit was "reproving and judging men."[3] He went on to say:

> This work of His had gone on until this point, aiming to correct and to check the strong propensity toward evil during the days of progressive degeneration. In spite of all the Spirit's corrective efforts "mankind" (*'adham*) had persisted in abandoning the way of truth and life. . . . Man is no longer simply sinful, as he has been right along since the Fall; the race has also as a whole practically sunk to the level of being flesh (*basar*), just plain, ordinary, weak and sinful stock, abandoned to a life of sin.[4]

> And God saw that the wickedness of man was great in the earth, and that every imagination of the thoughts of his heart was only evil continually.
>
> —Genesis 6:5

Leupold went on to point out that "two significant instances have told the whole story: the Sethites had grown indifferent to their heritage; the Cainites had developed high-handed violence."[5]

Jesus said, "But as the days of Noe were, so shall also the coming of the Son of man be" (Matthew 24:37). The Sethites picture the evangelicals of our day who have "grown indifferent to their heritage," having given up the old way of conversion, held by Baptists and Protestants before Charles G. Finney ruined evangelicalism in the last century.

Over 3,500 U.S. Churches Close Each Year!

If it seems that our conclusion is too strong, consider the following statistics, given by Woodrow Kroll, the director of Back to the Bible, in his book *The Vanishing Ministry*:

> Many American churches are not healthy. It is estimated that 80–85 percent of American churches have plateaued or are declining.
> The number of churches in America is not growing. In 1900

there were 27 churches for every 10,000 Americans. In 1985 this figure had declined so drastically that it is painful to report. There are now only 12 churches for every 10,000 Americans; less than half the former amount. Yes, this is the day of the super church, but even the phenomenon of the super church cannot account for this decline.

Add to this the number of churches that are now closing. There are over 66,000 closed churches in America. Another 62,000 are presently without pastors. **Between 3,500 and 4,000 churches close their doors each year in the USA.**

In 1900, 66 percent of the American population belonged to Bible-believing soul-winning churches. They all professed faith in Christ as Saviour. Yet it is predicted that by the year 2000 there will be only 33 percent of the American population who belong to a church.[6]

It should also be noted that the churches which do exist today are very often **not** Bible-believing. Many of them have become liberal since 1900. **The percentage of Americans who attend church has been cut in half since 1900, and many of the churches that still exist are not preaching the old gospel today.** This has happened, ironically, in a nation where the vast majority of the people claim to be saved.

Consider also the following poll, reprinted from the *Baptist Bible Tribune:*

BORN AGAIN CHRISTIANS IGNORANT OF FAITH
Survey Also Finds Hell's Description Divides American

GLENDALE, CA—The majority of born again Christians (87%) indicate their religious beliefs are very important in their lives today. However, claiming that religion's influence is significant doesn't necessarily translate into a personal faith consistent with biblical teaching. A new national survey of American adults by the Barna Research Group found that eight in ten (84%) born again Christians hold the non-biblical view on at least one of eight statements of biblical teaching tested in the survey.

"Born again Christians" are defined as individuals who say they have "made a personal commitment to Jesus Christ that is still important in [your] life today," and who chose one of seven alternatives posed regarding life after death. That alternative reads, "When you die you will go to Heaven because you have confessed your sins and have accepted Jesus Christ as [your] savior." Respondents were not asked to categorize themselves as "born again."

Survey Results

Born again Christians exhibit surprisingly high levels of ignorance on the following core Christian tenets:

- Eight in ten (80%) born again Christians agree with the statement, "The Bible teaches that God helps those who help themselves."
- Half (49%) agree with the statement, "The devil, or Satan, is not a living being, but is a symbol of evil."
- By definition all born again Christians believe they, personally, will go to heaven because they have "confessed their sins and accepted Jesus Christ as their savior." However, four in ten (39%) of the born again segment also maintain that "if a person is generally good, or does enough good things for others during their life, they will earn a place in heaven."
- Three in ten (30%) claim that "Jesus Christ was a great teacher, but he did not come back to physical life afer he was crucified."
- Twenty-nine percent contend that "when he lived on earth, Jesus Christ was human and committed sins, like other people."
- The same percentage (29%) assert that "there are some crimes, sins, or other things which people might do which cannot be forgiven by God."
- One-quarter (26%) disagree that "[they], personally, have a responsibility to tell other people [their] religious beliefs."
- Fifteen percent disagree that "the Bible is totally accurate in all of its teachings."

Bible Reading in the Survey

The survey findings also highlighted patterns in the Bible readership of Americans. One-third of all Americans (34%) have read from the Bible in the last seven days. That figure is essentially unchanged from the 1995 level, but reflects a sharp decline from 47% in 1992.

More than half of all born again Christians (57%) had read the Bible in the last week. Even among born again Christians, Bible readership is a shade lower than the percentage measured in 1993 (58%).

Americans' Views of Hell

The survey also found much disparity among Americans' views of Hell. Three in ten adults (31%) see Hell as an actual location: "a place of physical torment where people may be sent." Slightly more adults, nearly four in ten (37%), say "Hell is not a place, but it represents a state of permanent separation from the presence of God." Describing Hell as merely a symbolic term, not referring to a physical place, was true for two in ten Americans (19%). Ten percent of adults were undecided on their views of Hell.

This survey presents a dark picture of the Christianity in our nation.

The Days of Noah

We do not profess to know how large or small the number of truly born again Christians may be. From the various statistics we have given, however, the number seems to be small: "Except the Lord of hosts had left unto us a very small remnant, we should have been as Sodom, and we should have been like unto Gomorrah" (Isaiah 1:9).

Many have noticed that the spiritual condition of our generation is comparable to the days of Noah, but few have understood how this great apostasy came about in history. How did so many denominations, which formerly preached the Gospel, descend into apostasy in the last hundred years? How can such a large percentage of people claim to be saved today without believing the basic teachings of the Bible and without this having much of a positive effect on our crumbling society?

Churchill Saw Civilization Itself Crumbling

To answer these questions, we must go back in history. Winston Churchill, the British historian and statesman, had already noticed the decay of Western civilization when he made this statement during the "roaring twenties":

What a disappointment the Twentieth Century has been.
  How terrible and how melancholy
    is the long series of disastrous events
      which have darkened its first twenty years.
We have seen in every country a dissolution,
  a weakening of those bonds,
    a challenge to those principles
      a decay of faith
        an abridgement of hope
          on which the structure and ultimate existence
            of civilized society depends.[8]

He was right when he said that back in 1922. By 1935 Hitler was already on the march and Britain was suffering one humiliation after another. Churchill knew that Prime Minister Stanley Baldwin was too hopelessly weak to do anything about the growing Nazi menace. He recited in Parliament a poem from an 1883 edition of *Punch*, which he had memorized as a boy:

Who is in charge of the clattering train?
The axles creak and the couplings strain;
And the pace is hot, and the points are near,
And sleep has deadened the driver's ear;
And the signals flash through the night in vain,
For death is in charge of the clattering train.[9]

Prime Minister Baldwin was asleep at the throttle. A skeleton ran the train.

And that's the way it is again, sixty years later. Our culture is still clattering toward destruction. No strong, sure voice is heard to guide us. Our churches have either frozen to death in cold orthodoxy or fallen in a mass of laughter to the floor in so-called "laughing revivals" and "Brownsville awakenings."

Billy Graham Sees the Problem, But Not the Answer

Upon receiving the Congressional Gold Medal in May 1996, Billy Graham correctly said: "We are a society poised on the brink of self-destruction. Our culture is plagued with crime and violence, drug abuse, racial and ethnic tension, broken families and corruption."[10]

Yet Dr. Graham offers no solution other than another one of his crusades which, though given prime-time television exposure for close to fifty years, has contributed little to the solution, and is probably part of the problem. Western culture is rapidly declining into uncivilized savagery; our actions are primitive, caustic, cruel, and increasingly subhuman. Such a descent into barbarism did not come suddenly. We slid into it gradually over about fourteen decades. Dr. Martyn Lloyd-Jones spoke of "the terrible apostasy that has increasingly characterized the church for the last hundred years."[11]

The purpose of this book is to show how such apostasy came about and to do so in simple terms, understandable to the average man. Why is this important? Mainly because so many who think they are saved are actually going to Hell. Jesus said:

> Many will say to me in that day, Lord, Lord, have we not prophesied in thy name? and in thy name have cast out devils? and in thy name done many wonderful works? And then will I profess unto them, I never knew you; depart from me, ye that work iniquity.
>
> —Matthew 7:22–23

So many today have done a "wonderful work" of one sort or another, and therefore proclaim themselves saved. But "wonderful works," whether they be lifting the hand during an invitation, or saying the mere words of a sinner's prayer, will not save a human soul. "Depart from me. I never knew you." These are the words that await many thousands of people.

The true task of a preacher is to unmask the "wonderful works" of men and to reveal to them the fact that they are hopelessly lost sinners. That sort of preaching has brought anger and even violence, as illustrated in the days of Whitefield and Wesley, even down to our own day, when men like W. P. Nicholson and Duncan Campbell exposed religious-but-lost Protestants for what they were: sinners in the hands of an angry God.

The task of this book is to show how we got where we are and to give an answer in simple language. If we fail, we will at least have the consolation of having tried, which is far better than doing nothing in a day when "death is in charge of the clattering train."

Footnotes

1. M. R. DeHaan, *The Days of Noah* (Grand Rapids, MI: Zondervan Publishing House, 1963), p. 20.
2. Henry M. Morris, *The Genesis Record* (Grand Rapids, MI: Baker Book House, 1976), p. 154.
3. H. C. Leupold, *Exposition of Genesis* (Grand Rapids, MI: Baker Book House, 1976), p. 255.
4. Ibid.
5. Ibid., p. 260.
6. Woodrow Kroll, *The Vanishing Ministry* (Grand Rapids, MI: Kregel Publications, 1991), pp. 31–33.
7. *Baptist Bible Tribune,* April 15, 1996, p. 28.
8. Winston S. Churchill speech, recorded by Martin Gilbert, *Winston S. Churchill, Volume IV, World in Torment, 1917–1922* (London: William Heinemann, Ltd., 1975), pp. 914–15. When Churchill spoke, he did not use notes. Instead, he read the entire text of every speech. These speeches were typed out in broken lines to aid in delivery. Lord Halifax, followed by Churchill's staff, called this his "psalm form," because it looked like it was set down for singing.
9. William Manchester, *The Last Lion: Winston Spencer Churchill; Alone: 1932–1940* (Boston: Little, Brown, and Company, 1988), p. 148.
10. *Los Angeles Times,* May 3, 1996, p. A-10.
11. D. Martyn Lloyd-Jones, *Revival* (Wheaton, IL: Crossway Books, 1987), p. 57.

Chapter Two

The Monstrous Apostasy

Let no man deceive you by any means: for that day shall not come, except there come a falling away (apostasy) first. . . .
>　　　　　　　　　　　　　　　—2 Thessalonians 2:3

And many false prophets shall rise, and shall deceive many. . . .
>　　　　　　　　　　　　　　　—Matthew 24:11

These evils are destined to be propagated from generation to generation, waxing worse and worse.
>　　　　　　　　　　　　　　　—Dr. Asahel Nettleton
>　　1854 edition of *The Life and Labours of Asahel Nettleton*

One hundred and fifty years ago a wicked deception began, which grew in magnitude until it short-circuited revival and caused conversions to become a rare thing among evangelicals. Today we live in the burned-out aftermath, our churches either liberal, charismatic, or dead; our people claiming to be born again while missing church, divorcing, dancing, committing fornication, and aborting their babies. An increasing number of pastors commit adultery, while our youth go wild.

The monstrous apostasy surrounding us is a direct result of a theological transition which took place in the nineteenth century: a shift from conversion to decisionism. This book is about that change, and what we can do about it.

The stories given in this book are scrupulously true to the facts. They are given without the slightest embellishment. I say that at the beginning, because this first account seems too incredible to be true. But it is. I have known the man in this story for many years. This is exactly what happened.

A "Saved" Bank Robber

Like so many others I have talked to across the years, he had a vague uneasiness regarding his salvation. Nothing definite, nothing he could put his finger on, just a vague uneasiness. He told me that he had been saved years ago, but he couldn't say much about it. He had gone to a meeting with some friends. An invitation was given. He went forward. He made no mention at all of his sins, the blood of Jesus, or forgiveness. His whole testimony centered around the "decision" that he made years before.

He said that he had led a Christian group in high school. He had then become a Sunday school teacher in a Baptist church and later a deacon. He went through a divorce. Then he lost most of his money and his life fell apart. The thought went through his mind that he should rob a bank. He got out his old pistol. He planned it all carefully and walked into the bank and at gunpoint took all the money the teller could give him. The police caught him and he spent several months in prison.

I asked him, "What would have happened if the Rapture had come while you were holding the gun on that teller in the bank?" He stared at me with a sober face. Several seconds passed before he said, "The gun would have fallen to the floor and I would have been raptured."

I was never able to get him to move past a vague uneasiness to a place where he could see that the decision that he made years before was not a real conversion. The story of the man who thought that his pistol would fall to the ground and he would be raptured while robbing a bank illustrates what is wrong with so much of evangelicalism in our country. Yet many would say that this man was converted and would indeed have been raptured. Such is the sad state of religion in our time.

I knew this man as a dear friend from my childhood, when I first began attending church. I have loved him with all my heart. It tears me apart to see him go on clinging to a false hope, without a real conversion to give us hope of meeting together in Heaven some day. Many others have had a similar experience, which has inoculated them against real salvation. Oh God, save this man, and many others like him! Send a revival to sweep away the refuse of lies!

Did It Start with Jimmy Carter?

According to a recent Gallup poll, "Seventy-four percent of American adults eighteen and older say they have made a 'commitment' to Jesus Christ."[1] Yet our nation is morally and spiritually bankrupt. Speaking at a Bible conference I attended not long ago, one famous Baptist preacher said in my hearing, "Ever since President Carter, most people say they have been born again. They've learned to say it." I think he is partly correct, but the problem goes back farther than that, far back into the nineteenth century. It was a hundred and fifty years ago that a shift began to take place which gradually led to a change from conversions to mere "decisions for Christ."

In his book *Revival and Revivalism: the Making and Marring of American Evangelicalism 1750–1858,* Iain H. Murray points out that evangelicalism turned away from the old idea of conversion in the nineteenth century to the "decisionism" taught by Charles G. Finney (1792–1875). Murray declares that this transition was nearly complete in popular evangelical thinking by the beginning of the twentieth century:

> The idea that conversion is man's work became endemic to evangelicalism and, just as men forgot that regeneration is God's work, so belief in revival as the work of the Spirit of God disappeared. [This] was a direct product of Finney's theology.[2]

Murray's book gives deep insight into this pivotal period. Chapter fourteen should be read first. It outlines the slide of evangelical religion away from the old idea of conversion into Finney's new doctrine of "decisionism." Conversion as taught by the earlier Protestants and Baptists was gradually forgotten, replaced by a mere decision for Christ, whatever that meant to the individual. "Going forward," "raising the hand," "saying the sinner's prayer," "making Christ one's Lord," believing "the plan of salvation" or a few Bible verses, replaced the biblical idea of conversion as a work of God within the heart of man.

The change from conversion to decisionism, which was spearheaded by Finney, has been noticed by a number of others. David F. Wells, professor of historical and systematic theology at Gordon-Conwell Theological Seminary, has said, "The shift in understanding about conversion had several stages." He gave them and then pointed out that these changes are associated with Charles Finney's ministry.[3] The late historian William G. McLoughlin, Jr. spoke of "Charles Grandison Finney, who, in the years 1825–1835, created modern revivalism."[4] Evangelical theologian J. I. Packer agreed, saying that "evangelism of the modern type was invented by Charles G. Finney in the 1820s."[5] Richard Rabinowitz has written about the shift from conversion to decisionism during the time of Finney from a secular historian's viewpoint.[6] Other preachers had a part in this transition, but it was Finney who clearly led the way.

Thus, conversion was changed into decisionism largely through the ministry and writings of Charles G. Finney, as these men have pointed out. Finney's views engulfed the evangelical churches of America, and later, in the twentieth century, infiltrated many churches in the British Isles. Today, Iain Murray's statement is very nearly universal in the English-speaking world: "Men forgot that regeneration is God's work, so belief in revival as the work of the Spirit of God disappeared. [This] was a direct product of Finney's theology."[7] As William G. McLoughlin, Jr. put it, "He inaugurated a new era in American revivalism. He transformed the whole philosophy and process of evangelism."[8] We are still dealing with the effects of that transformation today. The apostasy around us reveals that Finney's decisionism has led to the death of our culture.

Although the nineteenth century English literary critic Matthew Arnold would not have understood it this way, his mournful dirge on the retreat of faith, given in the fourth stanza of his celebrated poem "Dover Beach," can be traced to the death of revival through decisionism:

> The Sea of Faith
> Was once, too, at the full, and round earth's shore
> Lay like the folds of a bright girdle furl'd.
> But now I only hear
> Its melancholy, long, withdrawing roar,
> Retreating, to the breath
> Of the night-wind, down the vast edges drear
> And naked shingles of the world.

We can be sure that the "melancholy, long, withdrawing roar" of faith, going out from us like the great tide at Dover Beach, will continue to slip away from our culture unless we repudiate Finney, his methods, and his supporters in the modern world.

Evangelicalism in Britain
British author Brian H. Edwards writes:

> I live in a borough of 132,000 inhabitants and I think I know most of the evangelical fellowship and churches among all the denominations; I also have an idea of the numbers that will be found worshipping among them each Sunday and it is hard to get much above one-and-a-half percent! And this is the so-called "Bible belt" of the southeast! I have discussed these statistics with Christians living in other towns, particularly in the north, where little more than a handful of believers meet week by week, and it would be difficult to muster one percent of the population in the evangelical commu-

nity. I know of one missionary who, during the 1970s, visited every home in a particular town in the northeast with a population of 80,000. He found only six evangelical Christian families; that is 0.015 percent! How the figure of seven percent was ever arrived at I do not know, but if it is accurate, then most evangelical Christians in the United Kingdom are unrecognizable during the week and keep well out of the way of Christian fellowship on Sunday.[9]

Thus, the situation in the United Kingdom is dark indeed. We are convinced that decisionist methods have eroded the churches of Britain as well as America. Though they have been far less inclined to use the public invitation, decisionism based on the mere affirmation of doctrine has harmed and emptied British churches in our time.

A Definition of Terms

What do we mean by decisionism? What do we mean by conversion? Here are working definitions of the two terms:

Decisionism is the belief that a person is saved by coming forward, raising the hand, saying a prayer, believing a doctrine, making a lordship commitment, or some other external, human act, which is taken as the equivalent to, and proof of, the miracle of inward conversion; it is the belief that a person is saved through the agency of a merely external decision; the belief that performing one of these human actions shows that a person is saved.

Conversion is the result of that work of the Holy Spirit which draws a lost sinner to Jesus Christ for justification and regeneration, and changes the sinner's standing before God from lost to saved, imparting divine life to the depraved soul, thus producing a new direction in the life of the convert. The objective side of salvation is justification. The subjective side of salvation is regeneration. The result is conversion.

Decisionism is on a human level. It counts something man does as the indication that conversion has occurred. Real conversion, on the other hand, is a saving encounter with the resurrected Christ.

Real conversion is, therefore, supernatural, while decisionism is purely human, carnal, and natural. Conversion is from God. Decisionism is from man. In decisionism a person does something which takes the place of a saving encounter with Jesus but is, in fact, not that at all. That is why so many people are unsaved today.

Historian Timothy L. Smith has pointed out these facts about Protestant and Baptist churches before Finney:

> **Certainly by modern standards church membership was a strenuous affair.** All evangelical sects required of communicants a personal experience of conversion and a consistent life. Two worship services and Sunday school on the Sabbath were customary, along with a midweek gathering for prayer. The Methodists* invariably kept new converts on "probation" for many months. . . . Laymen of most denominations were responsible for a large amount of missionary and benevolent work in the towns and cities. **All of these activities were pursued with a seriousness absent today.**[10]

After one hundred fifty years of Finney's "decisionism," the entire "seriousness" and commitment of early nineteenth century Protestantism is "absent." In fact, Gallup pollsters found "very little difference in the behavior of the churched and unchurched on a wide range of items including lying, cheating, and stealing."[11] Gallup concluded that "most people's religion is secondary."[12]

> They profess that they know God; but in works they deny him, being abominable, and disobedient, and unto every good work reprobate.
>
> —Titus 1:16

> Having a form of godliness, but denying the power thereof. . . .
>
> —2 Timothy 3:5

---

* And most other Protestant and Baptist churches, in varying degrees

According to a survey reported in the *Baptist Bible Tribune*, thirty percent of those who claim to be born again believe that "Jesus was a great teacher, but he did not come back to physical life after he was crucified."[13] Thus, at least one-third of those claiming to be born again are lost, since the Bible plainly says they are (1 Corinthians 15:17; Romans 10:9). No one can be born again who does not believe in the bodily resurrection of Jesus. The survey also found that eighty-four percent of born again Christians "hold the non-biblical view on at least one of eight statements of biblical teaching."[14]

It has been my impression, after hearing countless testimonies, that a large number of those who attend evangelical churches every Sunday are lost people, including Sunday school teachers, deacons, pastor's wives, and even pastors themselves. Dr. B. R. Lakin used to say that seventy-five percent of those attending Bible-believing churches were lost.[15] Dr. A. W. Tozer gave an even more dismal figure when he said, "Among evangelical churches probably no more than one out of ten know anything experientially about the new birth."[16] Evangelical author Paris Reidhead wrote:

> We've got to recognize that the message of salvation must not be addressed only to "the world," but to members of America's evangelical churches also. The greatest field for evangelism today, and in the days ahead, is among church members.[17]

Getting Evangelicals Saved

Some time ago, when preaching in an eastern state, I gave a strong sermon on the text, "Why will ye die?" (Ezekiel 33:11). At the invitation, seven men came forward. One of them was the associate pastor of the church. He had tears in his eyes, and he came with another man. I assumed that he was bringing this man to the front. However, I soon found out that the associate pastor was coming to be saved himself. He said that he was religious, but lost. As he spoke to me later he said, "I wonder how many others have made a decision without knowing what they were doing?"

In another meeting, I spoke on Matthew 7:21–23. The next day I went soul-winning with a young seminary student who had heard my sermon the night before. He told me that he had been afraid all day that they were going to team me up with him. I asked him why this frightened him. He said, "Because I know I'm lost." He was driving, so I said, "Pull over." He parked the car and I asked him to tell me his story. He said that he had been an active Catholic. He came to a Baptist church, brought by a friend, and went forward at the invitation. They baptized him. He told me that he had gone forward out of concern, but that he had never known Jesus Christ. The Christ he described to me was the angry judge (the Pantocrator) of the Roman Catholic Church, not the loving and forgiving Jesus of the Bible. I showed him the difference from the Scriptures. He saw it. He realized that he had never come to the real Jesus spoken of in the Bible. He was hopefully converted that night in the car.

Imagine what would have happened to him if he had graduated from seminary and gone out as a Baptist missionary trying to obey an angry Catholic "Christ." Think of how many people would have been confused by him on the mission field. Thank God he seemed to experience real conversion, instead of a mere decision, before he was sent out to the mission field!

In the next service, the man's wife sat listening to me preach with a strange look in her eyes. Her face went white and she stared straight ahead during the sermon. When the invitation was given she came forward. Everyone was shocked. She had been a teacher in the Christian school for several years. She told me that she had repeated the sinner's prayer when she was a small child, but had never thought of Jesus forgiving her sins. After dealing with her for a few minutes in private, she seemed clearly to have passed from death to life in true conversion.

Our critics may say that we believe people have "to get saved again." But we do not believe this. We are convinced that the Scripture teaches, "Once saved, always saved." **But many have never been saved in the first place!** Any charge that we think people have "to get saved again" will not be based on what we have written here, because that is not what we believe. We **do** believe that the methods of decisionism have ruined the churches and come near to destroying our nation and the English-speaking world.

Squeeze My Hand to Get Saved

I met one decisionist preacher at a Bible conference. He held out a little leather datebook as I shook his hand. An odd smile crossed his lips as he said, "Seven thousand saved last year." Later I heard a story about this preacher from a certain pastor. This decisionist is in the habit of "leading people to Christ" as he goes down the street and into the stores. He numbers them in his count of "conversions." In one grocery store he reached out and took a worker's hand in his. He said, "If you want to accept Christ, just squeeze my hand." The man gently pressed his palm, and the decisionist said, "Praise the Lord!" The worker was counted as one of his decisions for that week. A few days later the pastor of the local church went back to the store to follow up on the man. He said, "I'm really glad you got saved the other night." The man looked at him quizzically and finally said, "No hablo Ingles." That made it quite clear that this "decision" was from a Spanish-speaking man who did not understand a word of English, and therefore could not have been converted by the English-speaking decisionist!

Many of these decisionist preachers are being used far less in evangelistic meetings today because pastors see that they do not actually add people to the local church. The main reason they fail to add people to the churches is because they work for "decisions" rather than conversions. Local church pastors need to find ways to actually add people. If they join the church in an unconverted state they generally leave for some reason in a short time or, if they stay, cause trouble of one sort or another. We need to find ways to get more true converts to attend our churches. This book is written in an attempt to help fill that need.

By speaking personally to people in private, I have discovered that many have not understood the Gospel. They have raised their hand, said the sinner's prayer, or come forward, but they have not trusted Jesus in a real conversion experience.

So many people have been added to church rolls through decisions rather than conversions that the churches are now full of lost people, including lost church leaders and pastors themselves.

There has been no major national revival since 1859, and no great regional revival since the 1905 Welsh revival was felt in many parts of the English-speaking world. This situation has come about largely because God cannot and will not bless the false doctrines of decisionism, in my judgment.

Martyn Lloyd-Jones wrote:

> I have no hesitation in asserting that the main cause of the state of the Christian church today, and the whole state of the world, in consequence, is the terrible apostasy that has increasingly characterized the church for the last hundred years. And therefore, we have started with this: we have to get rid of this rubbish. . . . What makes us Christians? The work of regeneration; the Holy Spirit of God doing a work down in the very depths of the personality and putting there a principle of life, something absolutely new, so that there is a "new man."[18]

Dr. Lloyd-Jones was saying that we must get rid of decisionism and replace it with old-fashioned conversions before we can have true revival and actually add more solid people to our churches.

Bible Facts or Jesus Himself?

How do people get converted? It is not by learning a neat set of doctrines and Bible verses, either in a Catholic catechism class or a Baptist Sunday school. Conversions do not come by Bible knowledge alone. The Bible says, ". . . The holy scriptures, which are able to make thee wise unto salvation through faith which is in Christ Jesus" (2 Timothy 3:15). The Scriptures point us to Christ. Salvation is only in Christ. Believing the Bible, as an end in itself, does not save anyone. I believed every word of the Bible for several years before I was saved. Conversion did not occur until I encountered the resurrected Jesus. That is quite different from believing Bible facts **about** Jesus in nothing more than a decision.

Pollster George Gallup, Jr., has said, "The basic underlying problem is biblical illiteracy." Gallup identified this lack of knowledge as the biggest problem facing our churches today.[19] But he is **dead** wrong on this point. It is not biblical illiteracy that is at fault. It is the fact that people do not know Jesus Christ, **Himself.** Knowledge of Bible stories and even Bible memorization never saved anyone. The Jehovah's Witnesses usually know the Bible quite well, but they do not know Jesus, Himself.

The Bible was not nailed to the cross. The Bible does not sit at the right hand of God interceding for us. The Bible is God's inspired, inerrant Word **pointing** us to Jesus Christ. He alone is the Savior. Second Timothy 3:15 clearly tells us that the Bible directs us to Jesus for salvation.

There are thousands who have basic Bible knowledge but do not know Jesus Christ, Himself. I was one of them. I had been to Sunday school for over seven years. I had memorized more than one hundred twenty-five verses of salvation Scripture. I had memorized the facts of the Gospel. I even preached the Gospel. In fact, I was a licensed Southern Baptist preacher, but I did not know Jesus Christ personally. You see, I had gone to a service with a friend. I followed him when he went forward. It was my first time in a Baptist church. They baptized me in a white robe, but no one spoke to me about conversion. I was accepted for baptism based upon my decision of going forward. As a result, I spent seven miserable years as a lost Southern Baptist. I passed out Gospel tracts, preached a memorized Gospel, and was even licensed as a Baptist preacher while I was still lost. Without the grace of God, I would have gone on in the ministry unconverted. I am convinced that thousands of other preachers have never experienced a real conversion. They are in the same state I was in for those seven years. They are religious, but lost. I know what it's like from personal experience.

Footnotes

1. *National and International Religion Report,* October 8, 1990, p. 8.
2. Iain H. Murray, *Revival and Revivalism: the Making and Marring of American Evangelicalism 1750–1858* (Edinburgh: Banner of Truth Trust, 1994), pp. 412–13.
3. David F. Wells, *Turning to God:Biblical Conversion in the Modern World* (Grand Rapids, MI: Baker Book House, 1989), p. 93.
4. William G. McLoughlin, Jr., *Modern Revivalism: Charles Grandison Finney to Billy Graham* (New York: The Ronald Press Company, 1959), p. 11.
5. J. I. Packer, *A Quest for Godliness* (Wheaton, IL: Crossway Books, 1990), p. 292.
6. Richard Rabinowitz, *The Spiritual Self in Everyday Life:The Transformation of Personal Religious Experience in Nineteenth-Century New England* (Boston: Northeastern University Press, 1989).
7. Iain H. Murray, *Revival and Revivalism,* same as footnote 2.
8. McLoughlin, p. 11.
9. Brian H. Edwards, *Revival! A People Saturated with God* (Durham, England: Evangelical Press, 1991), pp. 15–17.
10. Timothy L. Smith, *Revivalism and Social Reform: American Protestantism on the Eve of the Civil War* (New York: Harper, 1965), p. 18.
11. Los Angeles *Herald Examiner,* July 14, 1984, p. 24.
12. Ibid.
13. "Born Again Christians Ignorant of Faith," *Baptist Bible Tribune,* April 15, 1996, p. 28.
14. Ibid.
15. Quoted by Roy L. Branson in *Dear Abner, I Love You. Joab* (Bristol, TN: Landmark Publications, 1992), p. 298.
16. A. W. Tozer, quoted by Paris Reidhead in *Getting Evangelicals Saved* (Minneapolis, MN: Bethany House Publishers, 1989), p. 46.
17. Paris Reidhead, *Getting Evangelicals Saved* (Minneapolis, MN: Bethany House Publishers, 1989), p. 47.
18. D. Martyn Lloyd-Jones, *Revival* (Wheaton, IL: Crossway Books, 1987), pp. 55–57.
19. Los Angeles *Daily News,* July 2, 1994, p. 19.

Chapter Three

Lost Preachers and Great Revivals

. . . In the last days perilous times shall come. For men shall be lovers of their own selves . . . Having a form of godliness, but denying the power thereof. . . .

—2 Timothy 3:1, 2, 5

It is an important part of a preacher's duty to discriminate between true and false conversions.

—Dr. Asahel Nettleton

The man who adds a profession of Christ to his own morality is the most difficult to convince of his unsound profession because he is among the most deceived of all men.

—William C. Nichols

I have . . . preached the doctrines of grace for a long time. But I believe I have never felt the power of them in my own soul.

—An old pastor speaking to George Whitefield.

George Whitefield, the powerful evangelist of the First Great Awakening, called Gilbert Tennent and his brothers "the burning and shining lights of this part of America."[1] Gilbert Tennent based his ministry on that of Whitefield. In 1741 Tennent published a sermon titled "The Danger of an Unconverted Ministry, Considered in a Sermon on Mark 6:34." This sermon had a far-reaching effect. It was based on the text, "And Jesus, when he came out, saw much people,and was moved with compassion toward them, because they were as sheep not having a shepherd" (Mark 6:34). This sermon was published many times and was popular for more than a century.[2] Here are several key paragraphs from "The Danger of an Unconverted Ministry":

What was the cause of this great and compassionate commotion in the heart of Christ? It was because He saw much people as sheep, having no shepherd. Why, had the people no teachers? Oh, yes! they had heaps of Pharisee-teachers. But notwithstanding of the great crowd of these orthodox, letter-learned, and regular Pharisees, our Lord commenced the unhappy case of that great number of people, who, in the days of His flesh, had no better guides: because that those were as good as none (in many respects) in our Saviour's judgment. For all them, the people were as sheep without a shepherd. The most notorious branches of their character were these, viz. Pride, Policy, Malice, Ignorance, Covetousness, and Bigotry to human inventions in religious matters.

Although some of the old Pharisee-shepherds had a very fair and strict outside; yet they were ignorant of the new birth: Witness Rabbi Nicodemus, who talked like a fool about it (see John 3:1-21).

Hear how our Lord cursed these plaistered hypocrites, Matthew 23:27, 28: "Woe unto you, scribes and Pharisees, hypocrites! for ye are like unto whited sepulchres, which indeed appear beautiful outward, but are within full of dead men's bones, and of all uncleanness. Even so ye also outwardly appear righteous unto men, but within ye are full of hypocrisy and iniquity." They were presently put into the priest's office, though they had no experience of the new-birth. O sad!

They came into the priest's office for a piece of bread; they took it up as a trade, and therefore endeavored to make the best market of it they could. O shame.

The Pharisees were fired with a party-zeal; they compassed sea and land to make a proselyte; and yet when he was made, they made him twofold more a child of hell than themselves. Paul himself, while he was a natural man (unconverted man), was wonderful zealous for the traditions of the fathers.

Natural men (unconverted men) have no call of God to the ministerial work under the gospel-dispensation. Isn't it a principal part of the ordinary call of God to the ministerial work, the aim of the glory of God, and in subordination thereto, the good of souls, as their chief marks in undertaking that work? And can any natural man (unconverted man) on earth do this? No! No!

Natural men (unconverted men), not having true love for Christ and the souls of their fellow-creatures, hence their discourses are cold and sapless, and as it were freeze between their lips. And not being sent of God, they (lack) that divine authority, with which the faithful ambassadors of Christ are clothed.

And Pharisee-teachers, having no experience of a special work of the Holy Ghost, upon their own souls, are therefore neither inclined to, nor fitted for, discoursing, frequently, clearly, and pathetically, upon such important subjects (as conversion).

They have not the courage, or honesty, to thrust the nail of terror into sleeping souls; nay, sometimes they strive with all their might, to fasten terror into the hearts of the righteous, and so to make those sad, whom God would not make sad!

They keep driving, driving, to duty, duty, under this notion, that it will recommend natural men (unconverted men) to the favor of God, or entitle them to the promises of grace and salvation: and thus those blind guides fix a deluded world upon the false foundation of their own righteousness; and so exclude them from the dear Redeemer.

All the doings of unconverted men, not proceeding from the principles of faith, love, and a new nature, nor being directed to the divine glory as their highest end, but flowing from, intending to self, as their principle and end; are doubtless damnably wicked in their manner of performance, and do deserve the wrath and curse of a sin-avenging God.

The ministry of natural men (unconverted men) is for the most part unprofitable. Isn't an unconverted minister like a man who would learn (teach) others to swim, before he has learned it himself, and so is drowned in the act, and dies like a fool?

Look into the congregations of unconverted ministers, and see what a sad security reigns there; not a soul convinced that can be heard of, for many years together; and yet the ministers are easy; for they say they do their duty.

Such who are contented under a dead ministry, have not in them the temper of our Saviour they profess. It is an awful sign, that they are as blind as moles and as dead as stones, without any spiritual taste and relish. And alas! isn't this the case of multitudes?[3]

In this sermon Tennent said that many of the preachers of his day were unconverted.* I believe there is a widespread repetition of this sad state today because decisionism has replaced old-fashioned conversions. That is one of the reasons some preachers may repudiate this book. Such unconverted preachers may rail against the truth as Paul did before he was saved.

Some time ago I invited a man to speak in our church. I thought it might be good for him to give his testimony before he preached. I asked him to give his testimony to Dr. Cagan and me in my office before the service. He told me that his mother had "led him to Christ" at three or four years old, but he had no memory of it. He said that he sometimes wondered if he were saved. Whenever these doubts came to him, he would phone his mother and she would assure him that **she** remembered his salvation. Here is a man whose assurance of salvation depended on his mother's memory! Here is a man that could not remember the most important event in his life!

---

* We have only given a few key paragraphs from "The Danger of an Unconverted Ministry." For the complete sermon, see pages 375 through 404 in *Sermons of the Log College,* compiled by Archibald Alexander (Ligonier, PA: Soli Deo Gloria Publications reprint, 1993) or *The Great Awakening: Documents Illustrating the Crisis and Its Consequences* (Old Tappan, NJ: Bobbs-Merrill, 1967), pp. 72–99.

I did not comment. As we went to the pulpit, I told him (as politely as possible) that he had best give the sermon without the testimony. I fear that there are others who are depending on a decision they cannot even remember, or a decision made from a wrong motive, or with wrong doctrine, or with a false hope at its base. Such "decisions" will not save preachers or anyone else from Hell.

Is the Holy Spirit's Work Satanic?

Sadly, it is quite common for preachers to give false assurance to lost people in our day. David Wilkerson, pastor of Times Square Church in New York City, gives a typical example:

> Who told you that you are unworthy—no good, unusable to God? Who keeps reminding you you're weak, helpless, a total failure? Who told you you'll never measure up to God's standard? We all know where this voice comes from: It is the devil himself![4]

We have heard statements like this often, but do they hold up in the light of Scripture? I don't think so. Men who take Wilkerson's position usually appeal to Revelation 12:10 to support their view that it is the devil who tells people that they are sinful. But Revelation 12:10 **doesn't say that Satan accuses people to themselves!** It says, "Which accuses them before our God." As Satan accused Job before God (Job 1:6–12), he will accuse the Tribulation saints "before God."

There is nothing in Revelation 12:10 which says that the devil tells people "they don't measure up to God's standard." That is the work of the **HOLY SPIRIT.** Jesus said: "And when he is come, he will reprove the world of sin, and of righteousness, and of judgment" (John 16:8).

It's dangerous to attribute the work of God's Spirit to Satan (Mark 3:22–30). I believe that Wilkerson's position can lead to blaspheming the Holy Ghost, by attributing His work to the devil. Once a person does this he has probably committed the unpardonable sin. It is virtually impossible to get people saved who habitually attribute conviction of sin to the devil. Yet many decisionist preachers actually encourage people to resist God's Spirit in this way. The preacher who gives false assurance and teaches people that it is Satan who convicts them of sin is actually helping the devil to damn souls.

The real situation is this: the Holy Spirit must strip the unconverted person of his pride and reveal to him that he is no good, unusable to God, a total failure, who will never measure up to God's standards. Unless the Holy Spirit does that, the sinner will never be converted in the true, biblical sense.

Let us compare Wilkerson's decisionist statement with that of Dr. Asahel Nettleton (1783–1843). Nettleton was the last major evangelist to oppose decisionism. He came out strongly against the "measures" used by Charles G. Finney. Let us compare what Nettleton, the classical evangelist, said with the modern, decisionist statement of David Wilkerson. Wilkerson said:

> Who told you that you are unworthy—no good, unusable to God? Who keeps reminding you you're weak, helpless, a total failure? Who told you you'll never measure up to God's standard? We all know where this voice comes from: It is the devil himself!

Nettleton said:

> The devil never awakened a sinner to a sense of his sins, guilt, and danger, but always tries to soothe and quiet him in his sins. If he can but keep him quiet, he knows that he is safe in his possession.[5]

Both positions cannot be right. You decide which statement best squares up with John 16:8.

In another place, Nettleton said:

> The devil will do all in his power to keep possession. By his subtlety he keeps sinners in peace. So long as the adversary of souls can

make the sinner believe that he is not lost, . . . he knows that he will not feel his need of salvation.[6]

Unconverted Preachers Get Saved

Between 1738 and 1770 George Whitefield made seven journeys from England to America, preaching from Georgia to New Hampshire and Maine. In one seventy-five–day period he preached one hundred seventy-five times and traveled eight hundred miles:

> At none of the meetings was there any "invitation." Whitefield merely preached and then waited for the Spirit to move. There were no counselors, no decision cards. When people were converted they made it known later. Ministers were among the converts. At dinner with young ministers in Stanford, Connecticut, Whitefield spoke vigorously against the practice of sending unconverted persons into the ministry. Two ministers, with tears in their eyes, publicly confessed that they had laid hands on young men who were unconverted. After the dinner, one old minister called Whitefield aside. Speaking with difficulty through his tears he said, "I have been a scholar and have preached the doctrines of grace for a long time. But I believe I have never felt the power of them in my own soul."[7]

Two main points can be noted from this quotation. First, many of the preachers, like this elderly man, were unsaved themselves and came to experience true conversion. Second, no evangelistic meetings before Charles Finney had any sort of "public invitation." The public invitation was never extended in the Great Awakening. None of the Puritans ever asked people to come forward or raise their hand. No Baptist ever did this before Finney. And the great "Prince of Preachers," Charles Spurgeon, never allowed an invitation in his church and never gave one himself. The "invitation" to come forward or raise one's hand to be saved came out of the methods used by Charles G. Finney and was virtually unheard of before 1830. The misuse of the invitation has led to "decisionism" instead of conversion.

Now, I personally do not believe that decisionism can be cured merely by giving up the invitation. I believe that people can be and are saved during public invitations. I give a public invitation in our church. People are saved using this method. It is not the invitation (if given correctly) which leads people astray. It is what we do after they respond that is crucial. We are suggesting careful personal work with the lost after the sermon by the pastor himself.

How Great Revivals Started
Eric W. Hayden, in his book *Spurgeon on Revival*, said this:

> Almost every book dealing with a spiritual awakening or a revival of history begins by describing the pre-revival situation in approximately the same words. For instance, you will read such words as these: "the darkness before the dawn"; "the sleep of midnight and gross darkness"; or "dissolution and decay." W. T. Stead, who was a child of the Welsh Revival of 1859, when writing of the later revival in the twentieth century, said of it: "Note how invariably the revival is preceded by a period of corruption."[8]

Many evangelicals today pray for revival and some even preach for revival. But few see that virtually every revival begins with the conversions of those who thought they were already saved. This was true of the First Great Awakening, the Second Great Awakening, and the Third Great Awakening of 1858–61. It was true of the revival on the Island of Lewis (1949–53), the last major regional revival in the English-speaking world. It has been true in nearly every classical revival on earth.

Duncan Campbell, who preached during the revival on the Island of Lewis, said this: "If you want revival, get right with God. If you are not prepared to bring the 'last piece' [of your life], for God's sake stop talking about revival. Your talking and praying is but the laughing stock of devils."[9]

The Jewish people who were converted in the book of Acts thought they were saved before they were converted. They thought they were saved by Jewish ritual and Jewish prayers, just as evangelicals today think they are saved by the rituals and prayers of "decisionism." In every classical revival those who thought they were saved have been converted. Their true conversions have ushered in revival. When the next revival begins in our culture it will almost certainly be among professed Christians who have made decisions but have not been converted.'

A thumbnail sketch of the history of revivals reveals that this thesis is true: revivals generally begin with the conversion of the religious, but lost. Other things also accompany the beginnings of revival, such as earnest prayer, but revivals usually have their first tangible fruits in the conversion of those who thought they were saved already.

The Jews in the book of Acts thought they were already saved, and often vigorously opposed the preaching of the apostles for this reason. Revival came as these lost Bible-believers, such as Paul, broke down and turned fully to Jesus in biblical conversion.

The great Protestant revival of the sixteenth century began with the conversion of Luther, who had been religious but lost for many years. Luther's conversion from dead Christianity was a birth-pang of the great Reformation revival. As James Burns points out, "The Reformation was supremely a revival. It marked for a vast multitude the recovery of faith."[10] Gilbert Egerton, a Belfast minister, has said:

The Reformation was a great and general revival of religion during which tens of thousands of souls were born again.This gracious spiritual awakening profoundly affected Germany, Switzerland, France, Holland, and Great Britain, also to a considerable degree Spain and Italy. The saving truths of the Word of God became so widespread and deeply rooted in the hearts of the people, that the Church of Rome tried in vain to halt its progress by kindling the fires of persecution. Without doubt the Protestant Reformation in the sixteenth century was the greatest revival of religion that the Church witnessed since the days of the Apostles.[11]

This revival began with the true salvation experience of Luther, a man already in the church, a man who was religious but lost, finding the reality of biblical conversion.

The revival in eighteenth century England really had its roots in the remarkable conversion of George Whitefield. He was already studying for the ministry and was a deeply religious young man, who spent hours in prayer and other Christian duties. But he was lost by his own admission. When he could no longer bear Christianity without Christ, he threw himself on his bed and cried out until Jesus came and saved him. Not long after this, his friends John and Charles Wesley were converted from dead Protestantism as well. And it was the conversion of these three religious but lost men that marked the beginning of this revival, which Burns called, "one of the most important events in modern religious history."[12]

The Great Awakening in New England began in the church pastored by Jonathan Edwards. Again, these were church people. The revival that swept New England began with the religious but lost people in Edwards' church experiencing true conversion.

This is an aspect in the history of revivals which has been largely overlooked, but it deserves deep study. Perhaps some day a whole book will be written on the history of revivals, showing how the vast majority of them began with the true conversions of people in the churches—people who already considered themselves Christians.

Northern Ireland—An Example

Here is a synopsis of the beginning of the 1859 revival as it came to northern Ireland, from a book by Dr. Ian R. K. Paisley:

> Without doubt, the first springing up of that mighty river of God . . . was in Antrim. In November 1856 a Mrs. Colville, an English lady, visited Ballymena. She had been religious but unregenerate, then one day the grace of God visited her, bringing salvation to her heart. She became a missionary of the Baptist Missionary Society in England. Her work brought her to Ulster and to the County Antrim.

One day she visited a home where a young woman lay dying. She described the nature of true conversion. Her words were overheard by a young man named James McQuilken. Mr. McQuilken feared that Mrs. Colville was not teaching straight Calvinistic doctrine. She replied, "I do not care to talk on mere points of doctrine. If one were to tell me what he knows of the state of his heart towards God, I think I could tell him whether he knows the Lord Jesus savingly." A woman who was present then began to unbosom herself to Mrs. Colville. Her spiritual condition was so much like that of James McQuilken that he felt as though he could not have described his own condition more perfectly. After a brief pause, [Mrs. Colville] said, "My dear, you have never known the Lord Jesus." [McQuilken] felt that this was true concerning himself, and the reply sent conviction like a dagger to his heart. After weeks of struggling under great agony of soul, he at last found peace and rest through trusting Jesus.

Jeremiah Meneely was a communicant member of Connor Presbyterian Church, but he could not claim such a knowledge of sins forgiven [as McQuilken did]. Meneely sought out James McQuilken. The glorious light burst into his heart and the same peace which his friend had experienced became his, too.

During the long winter of 1857–1858 every Friday evening, these young men . . . poured out their prayers. . . . As the revival rose, the old schoolhouse was crowded out.[13]

That is the way the 1859 revival came to northern Ireland. Like the vast majority of revivals, it began with a few people (three people in this case), a Baptist woman and two Presbyterian men, who had been religious but lost. When the next revival comes, it will almost certainly come the same way, by church members who proclaim themselves saved becoming undone and then converted.

We have had no major revival for over ninety years largely because pastors are content with "decisionism," in my judgment, and àre afraid to say to their people what Mrs. Colville said after hearing a woman's testimony, "My dear, you have never known the Lord Jesus." This Baptist woman was then used by God in the conversion of two Presbyterian men, and the revival began.

Was Mrs. Colville wrong when she told this woman her testimony was deficient? Did she violate Matthew 7:1, "Judge not, that ye be not judged"? No, she did not. The entire passage (Matthew 7:1–6) refers to people judging others for sins they themselves are committing (see verse 5). Mrs. Colville would only have been wrong, in the light of this entire passage, if she *herself* had not known the Lord Jesus. There is nothing wrong with someone who is truly converted telling a lost person that his testimony does not reveal saving faith, as Jesus and the apostles often did.

Nettleton Warned Against False Conversions

Today it is common for decisionists to say that no one can tell who is saved. I heard Billy Graham declare this on television recently. But Jesus often pointed out who was saved and who was lost. He told Nicodemus that he needed to be born again (John 3:7). He told the woman at the well, quite bluntly, that she did not have the water of life (John 4:10) and did not know God (John 4:22). He proclaimed Judas lost when He said, ". . . one of you is a devil . . ." (John 6:70). He told a group of men, ". . . I know you, that ye have not the love of God in you" (John 5:42). To another such group, He said, ". . . Ye are of your father the devil . . ." (John 8:44). He also knew when people were saved, such as Zacchaeus (Luke 19:9), the woman who kissed His feet (Luke 7:50), the thief on the cross (Luke 23:43), and others. Peter told Simon the sorcerer that he was lost (Acts 8:21–23) although he had already been baptized and had belief in doctrines about Christ, without conversion (Acts 8:13). Paul called some who said they were saved "false brethren" in 2 Corinthians 11:26 and Galatians 2:4. Christians in general are told not to be ". . . unequally yoked together with unbelievers . . ." (2 Corinthians 6:14). This requires that every Christian must have enough sense, in general, to know who is saved and who is not. So, Billy Graham is not true to the Scriptures when he states that no one can tell us who is saved and who isn't.

The old preachers could tell, by listening to the testimony of inquirers. Asahel Nettleton gave a typical pre-Finney example of how preachers examined the testimonies of the lost.

> When any indulged in a hope which was not satisfactory, he would say: "You had better give it up, and seek your salvation in earnest." Well versed in all the doctrinal and experimental parts of the Gospel . . . he was qualified to judge of the character of others' experience; and though mild and conciliatory in his manner, he was faithful in his warnings against false hopes and spurious (false) coversions.[14]

The old preachers, like Dr. Nettleton, were willing to say words such as, "My dear, you have never known the Lord Jesus," to those who had deficient testimonies.

Rejection of Nettleton's Methods Produced Today's Modernism, Charismatism, and Dead Conservatism

Asahel Nettleton became an evangelist after his graduation from Yale University in 1812. Over the next ten years he saw revival break out nearly everywhere he preached. It is estimated that over thirty thousand people were genuinely converted through his brief ministry. In that day, this could only mean union with the local church, not mere decisions by people never heard from again. Thirty thousand people actually joined the churches and stayed in them as a result of his rather short ministry. He strongly opposed the decisionism of Charles G. Finney.

Nettleton's method was to preach on Sunday and on one or two weeknights in a local church. His sermons were mostly on Hell, death, the final judgment, reprobation, and total depravity. He would make himself available during the week for awakened sinners to see him in private. He often counseled people a number of times prior to their conversion.

Asahel Nettleton frequently reminded his hearers of the signs of genuine conversion and warned those who heard him to beware of thinking they were converted when they were not.[15]

Dr. Nettleton's methods were not new or unique. He followed

the general pattern laid out many years before by Richard Baxter in *The Reformed Pastor*. Nettleton's way was the old path. He took time with each inquirer. He often counselled people personally several times, until they had a true understanding of the Gospel and a real conversion. However, Nettleton was the last nationally-known American evangelist to stick strictly by the older methods.

Speaking of the new way of preaching brought in by Finney, Nettleton said:

> I have often been struck with this circumstance in the mode of preaching, that nothing was heard of the danger of spurious (false) conversion. For months together, the thought never seemed to be glanced at, that there was any such thing as a Satanic influence in the form of religion.[16]

This mistake is very nearly universal among evangelical preachers today, as a result of following Finney's methods.

Nettleton said: "It is of the highest importance that the preacher present to his hearers the distinguishing marks of true religion and at the same time, that he detect and expose their counterfeit."[17]

Again he said: "It is an important part of a preacher's duty to discriminate between true and false conversion. Without this, every discerning Christian knows that the work will rapidly degenerate."[18]

We have largely been without such discrimination for over a hundred years. We have certainly experienced degeneration as a result. Dr. Peter Masters, pastor of Spurgeon's Metropolitan Tabernacle in London, asked these probing questions:

> How did the scourge of modernism ever succeed in wiping out the true Gospel from so many western Protestant denominations over the last hundred years? And what caused countless evangelical churches to capsize before the tide of "worldly" Christianity which arose only three decades ago?[19]

Here is his answer: "In the history of the Christian Church the greatest problems have always stemmed from the presence of unsaved people in the church membership."[20]

For revival to come, we must preach: "Examine yourselves, whether ye be in the faith . . ." (2 Corinthians 13:5). And we must have the courage to preach this to lost church members.

O. Hallesby, whose book on prayer has been a blessing to many, has shown that such sharp preaching on self-examination is particularly important in our day, when so much evangelistic preaching focuses on the sins of people who are *not present*, such as drunkards, homosexuals, Mormons, or Catholics. He said:

> They very rarely come and listen. Our audiences usually consist of good people, moral folk, even religious people. And we make these people even more self-satisfied Pharisees than they are if we speak only of gross sins and do not attack their real sins, their inner sins, which are doubly difficult for these people to become aware of because of their moral life and their religion.[21]

We are saying that the greatest problem in the churches today comes from the large number of lost people who are members. And we are saying that nothing short of plain, sharp preaching, which causes these people to examine their own hearts, can be instrumental in paving the way for God, in His sovereign power, to send real revival.

There has been no major revival for over ninety years. From the human side, this is largely due to a lack of conscience-probing preaching directed toward lost evangelicals. Dr. Asahel Nettleton said: "That preaching which does not aim at the heart, and take hold of the conscience, never attacks the strong holds of Satan."[22]

William C. Nichols, modern publisher of Nettleton's sermons, points out that "the man who adds a profession of Christ to his own morality is the most difficult to convince of his unsound profession because he is among the most deceived of all men."[23] Since our churches are now full of such deceived individuals, a great deal of conscience-probing preaching on self-examination is needed at this time.

I cannot think of any more important subject in our day. Preachers need to know whether their people are converted. Church members need to examine themselves. Preaching needs to be directed toward the conscience. Those who are religious need to be directed toward self-examination. Our preaching needs to be very pointed in this time of apostasy.

Footnotes

1. Alan Heimert and Perry Miller, *The Great Awakening: Documents Illustrating the Crisis and its Consequences* (Old Tappan, NJ: Bobbs-Merrill, 1967) p. 71.
2. Ibid., p. 72.
3. Gilbert Tennent, "The Danger of an Unconverted Ministry," in *The Great Awakening: Documents Illustrating the Crisis and its Consequences* (Old Tappan, NJ: Bobbs-Merrill, 1967), pp. 72–99.
4. David Wilkerson, "Who Told You You Are Unworthy?", Times Square Church Pulpit Series, April 4, 1997 (published by World Challenge, Inc., Lindale, Texas), p. 1.
5. Asahel Nettleton, *Sermons from the Second Great Awakening* (Ames, IA: International Outreach, 1995 reprint), p. 160.
6. Ibid.
7. *America's Great Revivals*, pp. 16–17. Minneapolis: Bethany House Publishers, no date, no author. Reprinted from *Christian Life* magazine, copyrighted by *Sunday* magazine.
8. Eric W. Hayden, *Spurgeon on Revival*, (Grand Rapids, MI: Zondervan Publishing House, 1962), p. 39.
9. Duncan Campbell, *The Price and Power of Revival* (Belfast: The Faith Mission, n.d.), p. 29.
10. James Burns, *Revivals, Their Laws and Leaders* (Grand Rapids, MI: Baker Book House, 1969), p. 163.
11. Ian R. K. Paisley, *The Revivalist*, September, 1997, p. 19.
12. Burns, p. 283.
13. Ian R. K. Paisley, *The Fifty Nine Revival* (Belfast: Martyrs Memorial Free Presbyterian Church, 1987), pp. 14–19.
14. Bennet Tyler and Andrew Bonar, *The Life and Labours of Asahel Nettleton* (Edinburgh: Banner of Truth Trust, 1975; reprinted from the 1854 edition), p. 243.
15. Asahel Nettleton, *Sermons from the Second Great Awakening* (Ames, IA: International Outreach, 1995 reprint), foreword, i.
16. Bennet Tyler and Andrew Bonar, *The Life and Labours of Asahel Nettleton*, p. 367.
17. Ibid., p. 368.

18. Ibid.
19. Peter Masters, *Seven Certain Signs of True Conversion* (London: Sword and Trowel, 1976), p. 20.
20. Ibid.
21. O. Hallesby, "How Can the Word of God Be Preached So As to Result in Awakening and Conversion?" from *The Christian Life* by O. Hallesby (Augsburg Publishing House, 1962).
22. Asahel Nettleton, *Sermons from the Second Great Awakening*, i.
23. William C. Nichols, *The Narrow Way* (Ames, IA: International Outreach, Inc., 1993), p. 74.

Chapter Four

Invading Satan's Kingdom

... The devil is come down unto you, having great wrath, because he knoweth that he hath but a short time. ...

—Revelation 12:12

Some of the most vicious opposition to revival has come from the professing church.

—Brian Edwards

Nothing can be done toward recovering lost sinners to God without invading the kingdom of darkness.

—Dr. Asahel Nettleton

Examine yourselves because if ye make a mistake ye can never rectify it, except in this world. Well might the apostle say, "Examine yourselves."

—C. H. Spurgeon

To be sure, there is a great risk involved in old-time preaching and counselling. Agitation, flurries of backbiting, and outright church splits will often attend such ministry. How do we know? By reading the Bible and Christian history.

The Book of Acts describes one division after another across its pages. For instance, in Acts 4:2–4 some of the people believed, while the rest were grieved. The preaching of the apostles produced grief or belief. There was no middle ground. In Acts 13:48–50 there was a division of the people which resulted in the preachers being "expelled them out of their coasts." In Acts 14:4 we read: "But the multitude of the city was divided. . . ." In Acts 17:1–9 we read of certain people who were "moved with envy" who ". . . troubled the people and the rulers of the city, when they heard these things. . . ." When Paul preached at Ephesus, ". . . divers were hardened, and believed not, but spake evil of that way . . . he departed from them, and separated the disciples" (Acts 19:8–9). At Rome, ". . . some believed the things which were spoken, and some believed not . . ." (Acts 28:24).

Clear, plain preaching which caused people to examine their own salvation produced great division throughout the book of Acts, as the apostles followed the example set by Jesus in His own preaching ministry.

Jesus, Himself, quite often caused such division through His preaching (John 7:43; John 9:16; John 10:19). The last verse in this list, John 10:19, tells us: "There was a division therefore again among the Jews for these sayings." Jesus' sermon was so probing (He called them thieves and robbers in verse 1) that although they understood little of its spiritual content, it angered and divided them. In Luke 12:51 Jesus said: "Suppose ye that I am come to give peace on earth? I tell you, Nay; but rather division."

Dr. John R. Rice once said:

No need to blame Hollywood and the liquor and drug crowd for the mess we are in. Blame lies at the doorstep of sissy, compromising, back-scratching, ear-tickling preachers who know the truth yet refuse to preach it for fear of hurting someone's feelings. It is not inviting to be unpopular. No one likes to be shunned. It is not a good feeling to know you are not appreciated. But our Lord went through all that—and more. He set our example.[1]

Yes, the preaching of Jesus and His apostles produced divisions between the saved and the stubborn, hard-hearted lost. This has happened throughout Christian history to men who preached as Christ and the apostles did; men who made lost people examine themselves to see whether they were converted (2 Corinthians 13:5).

Remember that Luther was excommunicated from the Catholic Church for this reason. Remember that John Wesley wrote again and again in his journal, "I must preach there no more," when church after church closed to him, and he was finally forced out into the fields to preach because no church would have him in its pulpit. Remember that George Whitefield was bitterly lampooned on the stage and also driven from the churches for such preaching. Remember that Bunyan was put into prison for such preaching, and Jonathan Edwards was fired from his church for trying to get lost teenagers in his congregation converted.

Brian Edwards has said, "Some of the most vicious opposition to revival has come from the professing church."[2] He pointed out that "every church was closed to Bakht Singh," the great Indian evangelist.[3] At Cambuslang, Scotland, in 1742, the Associate Presbytery called George Whitefield "a limb of Anti-Christ," and spread "lies, slanderous reports, and ridiculous stories" to prejudice people against his preaching.[4] The Scottish evangelist Duncan Campbell was accused of hypnotizing people in the 1940s.[5] Evangelist Howel Harris of Wales declared, "I was almost murdered once, and twice in danger of my life, besides being before the Magistrate."[6] This sort of opposition to preaching for conversions is very nearly universal in history.

When we today take up the desperately needed task of preaching, "Examine yourselves, whether ye be in the faith," we must expect a response similar to that experienced by Jesus, the apostles, Luther, Wesley, Whitefield, Bunyan, Edwards, Wesley, Howel Harris, Bakht Singh, Duncan Campbell, and so many other faithful preachers. We must expect angry, hard-hearted, unconverted Protestants and Baptists to reject us, speak evil about us behind our backs, and put us out of their churches.

The man who is faithful to the Lord in his preaching must expect to be rejected in this time of apostasy. His true companions will be the faithful preachers of long ago. He will walk alone among the dead, his path described by the nineteenth century Irish poet Thomas Moore:

> I feel like one
> Who treads alone
> Some banquet hall deserted,
> Whose lights are fled,
> Whose garlands dead,
> And all but he departed.

The God-Called Preacher—Rare Today

I believe that one main reason there are so few old-time, sin-denouncing sermons today, is because many ministers have no clear calling to preach. Men who are not called by God to preach will give soothing Bible studies that don't disturb anyone; they will *not* preach like Howel Harris, Duncan Campbell, or John Bunyan. There must be a clear call from God for a man to preach like them.

On three separate occasions I can vividly remember God calling me to preach. God called me the second time directly after a youth leader censured and rebuked me for preaching against sin. I was seventeen years old. God Himself told me, in my heart, that this man was wrong, that I should continue to preach as I did. Later it was revealed that this "youth leader" was a pervert.

The third time I was called to preach, I was thirty-two years old and had been a student for two years at a Southern Baptist seminary. A liberal professor told me not to take a strong stand for the Scriptures. He said, "You're getting a bad reputation as a trouble-maker." I thought that over. I wanted to quit the ministry because I felt I couldn't speak out the way God had called me to do. Then, late at night, God called me to preach again. He spoke to my heart and plainly told me to go back to the seminary, uphold His Word, and preach hard against sin. I did get a reputation as a trouble-maker among the Southern Baptist liberals, but I have been greatly

blessed by God in my own family, home, and church. Such a reputation is not necessarily a bad one in a time of deep apostasy.

I know some men say that strong stands like this are not necessary in our day. I know they often say everything can be taken care
of "behind closed doors" now. They'll tell you that we no longer
need preachers like W. B. Riley, T. T. Shields, J. Frank Norris, or
Bob Jones, Sr. They say we can avoid controversy by secret nego-
tiations, but they are wrong. Sin cannot be exposed without controversy. Error cannot be corrected without controversy. Ask Paul.
Ask Luther. Ask Bunyan. Ask William Jennings Bryan. The old-
timers knew that a real preacher must stand for God's truth and
against error, even if it is controversial to do so, and even if the
preacher has to stand alone. The old-time preachers knew that,
even though their grandchildren may have forgotten it. No man
can preach the way God wants him to without ruffling someone's
feathers—without preaching against sin.

One reason men are afraid to preach against sin today is that
many of them have not been called to preach at all.

> I have not sent these prophets, yet they ran: I have not spoken to
> them, yet they prophesied.
>
> —Jeremiah 23:21

> I have seen also in the prophets of Jerusalem an horrible thing:
> they commit adultery, and walk in lies: they strengthen also the
> hands of evildoers, that none doth return from his wickedness: they
> are all of them unto me as Sodom, and the inhabitants thereof as
> Gomorrah . . . for from the prophets of Jerusalem is profaneness
> gone forth into all the land. . . .
>
> —Jeremiah 23:14–15

> I sent them not, nor commanded them: therefore they shall not
> profit this people at all, saith the LORD. . . .
>
> —Jeremiah 23:32

God-called preachers are the only ones who understand the need for old-fashioned preaching against sin.

C. H. Spurgeon said this about the men God calls to preach: "The word of God must be unto us as fire in our bones, otherwise, if we undertake the ministry, we shall be unhappy in it, shall be unable to bear the self-denials incident to it, and shall be of little service to those among whom we minister."[7]

Dr. E. C. Carrier once made this statement about the God-called preacher: "There is no way to explain his behavior apart from his calling."[8]

Dr. Roy Branson says: "To the unbeliever and the carnal Christian everything about a truly called preacher totally defies understanding or explanation."[9]

> The divinely called preacher gradually becomes aware of the fact that he has embarked on a whole new manner of life—a life for which he was born into this world, but of which he probably never dreamed before. All the goals of his life before his call become meaningless, discarded as ashes from last winter's fire. "I never felt that way," someone may protest. We can only reply with the kindliest intent, "You were never called of God. Please quit preaching."[10]

I repeat, only a God-called preacher will understand the need for preaching against sin. Those who have *not* been called will think he is odd. "Why not negotiate? Why be controversial? Why make a fuss?" These are the questions often asked by those with no clear calling to preach. But God-called preachers will instantly understand the answers to their questions. They will know intuitively why they must preach against sin. It is part of the enlightenment that goes with the calling.

Invading Satan's Kingdom

Asahel Nettleton said,

> Nothing can be done toward recovering lost sinners to God without invading the kingdom of darkness. The adversary is tenacious

of his subjects. Nothing can be done by the gospel without awakening his jealousy, and arousing his opposition. He will exert his power to the utmost to retain every soul in his kingdom. . . . When the devil tries to make sinners believe they are not lost, they try in turn to believe him. When others soothe and flatter and attempt to quiet their fears, and tell him that they need not be alarmed, there is no danger, they are pleased with it. Especially when they hear smooth things from the (pulpit), this is exceeding pleasant and useful and the most effectual means of helping on the work of fortifying the sinners' hearts against Christ. . . . When the solemn truths of God's word are declared in a clear and convincing manner, sinners are often alarmed. They are sometimes almost convinced, and begin to say, if these things be so, then my situation is truly alarming. . . . In this situation the sinner will seize with avidity every thing which may help him to condemn others and justify himself. If he cannot condemn the messages of divine truth, he feels an awful conviction.[11]

Most preachers want to avoid conflict. That is understandable. But conflict cannot be avoided if souls are to be converted. As Nettleton indicated, conflict with Satan and demonic forces is inevitable.

A preacher who is afraid of losing lost church members will not be able to enter into this sort of conflict with Satan. He will be afraid he might lose someone in his congregation.

One man said, "You don't understand. We can't preach like that any more. There are many churches where they can transfer." Such preachers feel trapped. They must now help Satan deceive the lost people in their congregations out of the fear of losing them. Satan uses this fear to enslave preachers and use them as his servants to help destroy the souls of their lost members.

Instead of being a strong man, preaching the truth of God, the pastor is reduced to a servant of Satan. In this way, the devil makes slaves of many preachers today. They are dominated and ruled by people in their own congregations, unconverted members who are used by Satan to manipulate and control the preacher. Unconverted wives of preachers can occupy this position, as well as others in the church. Such pastors become enslaved to the rulers of darkness, rather than fighting against them as they should, according to the Bible:

> Put on the whole armour of God, that ye may be able to stand against the wiles of the devil. For we wrestle not against flesh and blood, but against principalities, against powers, against the rulers of the darkness of this world, against spiritual wickedness in high places.
>
> —Ephesians 6:11–12

The work of true ministry is warfare with Satan and his angels. Paul recognized this in this exhortation to Timothy: "This charge I commit unto thee, son Timothy, according to the prophecies which went before on thee, that thou by them mightest war a good warfare" (1 Timothy 1:18).

"Thou therefore endure hardness, as a good soldier of Jesus Christ. No man that warreth entangleth himself with the affairs of this life; that he may please him who hath chosen him to be a soldier" (2 Timothy 2:3–4).

The work of a preacher is to wage war with the devil (cf. Ephesians 6:11–12). The man who fails to understand this will never preach the way he ought to, because he will not understand who he is opposing, how and through whom his opponent operates, or how to expose his enemy. He will not be able to invade the kingdom of darkness and recover lost sinners to God. Such preachers become unwitting tools in the hands of demons rather than warriors of the Spirit. Hear the words of Jeremiah to such a preacher: "The LORD hath not sent thee; but thou makest this people to trust in a lie; Therefore thus saith the LORD; Behold, I will cast thee from off the face of the earth" (Jeremiah 28:15–16).

Examine Yourself

We have prayed long decades for revival like that which came in

1859, but it has not been sent·to us. Why? We must first expose the demonic error of decisionism in all its forms. Satan will oppose the man who does this. The very name of Satan means "adversary," because he opposes the true work of the ministry. The God-called preacher must have enough moral courage and spiritual insight to preach, "Examine yourselves, whether ye be in the faith" (2 Corinthians 13:5; cf. 1 Corinthians 11:28). Preachers who are afraid of saying such things will *never* experience revival like that which came in 1859. They may hold on to a church, but they will not see revival in it.

> The price of revival, the cost of soul winning,
> The long hours of praying, the burden, the tears,
> The pleading with sinners, though lonely, a stranger,
> Is repaid at the reaping up there.
> —Dr. John R. Rice,

"The Price of Revival"

There are many praying people who could be blessed with revival, but not without courage, not without risk, not without cost. The preacher must be willing to say to a lost church member, "My dear, you have never known the Lord Jesus," as Mrs. Colville did at the beginning of the 1859 revival in northern Ireland.

Throughout Christian history leading preachers have taken our position on 2 Corinthians 13:5. The seventeenth century commentator Matthew Poole said of this verse: "He bids them to be very often and very seriously proving themselves, as to this thing, whether they be in Christ, and whether they have saving faith."[12]

Jonathan Edwards gave these comments on the verse:

> We should look upon it as of the greatest importance to us, to know in what state we are, whether we ever had any change made in our hearts from sin to holiness, or whether we be not still in the gall of bitterness and bond of iniquity; whether every sin were truly mortified in us; whether we do not live in the sin of unbelief, and in

the rejection of the Saviour. This is what the apostle insists upon with the Corinthians (2 Corinthians 13:5). Those who entertain the opinion and hope of themselves, that they are godly, should take great care to see that the foundation is right. Those that are in doubt should not give themselves rest till the matter be resolved.[13]

Albert Barnes wrote:

This examination, however, is never unimportant or useless for Christians; and an exhortation to do it is *always** in place. So important are the interests at stake, and so liable are the best to deceive themselves, that all Christians should be often induced to examine the foundation of their hope of eternal salvation.[14]

In a sermon titled, "Self-Examination," which was based upon 2 Corinthians 13:5, C. H. Spurgeon said:

Examine yourselves because if ye make a mistake ye can never rectify it, except in this world. . . . I cannot afford to have my soul cast into hell. What a frightful hazard is that which you and I are running, if we do not examine ourselves! It is an everlasting hazard; it is a hazard of heaven or hell, of God's eternal favor or of his everlasting curse. Well might the apostle say, "Examine yourselves."[15]

Twenty-six years after he gave that sermon, Spurgeon preached another one on 2 Corinthians 13:3–5 titled "The Proof of Our Ministry." In it he said:

A man cannot make too sure work about his own salvation. . . . We must again and again examine ourselves. If you do not test yourself you may sit down and say, "Oh, I am all right." Yes, but you may be fostering within your spirit a peace which will end in your final ruin, and you may never open your eyes to your deception till you lift them up in hell.[16]

---

* · Emphasis by Dr. Barnes.

Closer to our own day, evangelical Bible commentator J. Vernon McGee gave the same interpretation and application of 2 Corinthians 13:5:

Paul says we should examine ourselves to see whether we are in the faith or not. We should be willing to face up to the issue. I think two or three times a year we should do this. I think every believer ought to do that.[17]

Second Corinthians 13:5 is a key verse in our day. It should be preached and fearlessly applied by men who have the spirit of Bunyan, Edwards, and Whitefield. We may go through fierce conflict with Satan and his demons. We may be rejected and scorned for preaching such self-examination, but the results will be real conversions and, very possibly, real revival. Let us call upon the people in our congregations to indicate their willingness to obey 2 Corinthians 13:5. Let us then pray for them, as they obey the Word of God and examine themselves whether they be in the faith. Let us also preach sermons, like the old-time preachers did, which help complacent, lost church members reject their carnality and lay hold on the Son of God.

Asahel Nettleton, the nineteenth century evangelist who opposed Finney's decisionism, often called for professing Christians to examine themselves. In a sermon on 2 Corinthians 13:5, Dr. Nettleton said:

The duty enjoined in the text is no less important to us than it was to the Corinthians, and is as binding on professors of religion now, as in the days of the Apostles. . . . In this business, every individual must sit in judgment on himself. Deal faithfully with your souls. A false hope is worse than none. A mistake in this momentous concern is awful. Examine well the foundation on which you rest your hopes of heaven, lest you discover your mistake too late.[18]

We have prayed for decades for revival like that which came to America, Great Britain, and northern Ireland in 1859, but it has not come. Why the delay? Because we must first expose decisionism in all of its insidious and satanic forms, and be willing to tell lost church members, "My dear, you have never known the Lord Jesus," as Mrs. Colville did.

The Boneless Wonder

Many preachers today have become too cowardly to confront the lost in this way. They remind me of what Winston Churchill said in Parliament, about Prime Minister Ramsay MacDonald, in 1931. Churchill's description of this weak politician is a classic:

> I remember when I was a child, being taken to the celebrated Barnum's circus which contained an exhibition of freaks and monstrosities, but the exhibit on the programme which I most desired to see was the one described as "The Boneless Wonder." My parents judged that that spectacle would be too revolting and demoralizing for my youthful eyes, and I have waited fifty years to see the boneless wonder sitting on the Treasury Bench (the Prime Minister and his Cabinet).[19]

Like Prime Minister MacDonald, many preachers in our day have become "boneless wonders," too cowardly to preach against sin, too spineless to insist on conversion, too blind to see that the enemy is Satan.

Dr. J. Gresham Machen was a champion of fundamentalism. He also believed that modern preaching had gone wrong. Machen said:

> Modern preachers are trying to bring men into the Church without requiring them to relinquish their pride; they are trying to help men avoid the conviction of sin. . . . Such is modern preaching. It is heard every Sunday in thousands of pulpits. But it is entirely futile.[20]

D. Martyn Lloyd-Jones was pastor of Westminster Chapel in London for many years. He is considered one of the foremost authorities in the twentieth century on the subjects of revival and preaching. Like Machen, he also believed modern preaching had gone wrong. Lloyd-Jones said:

> Present-day preaching does not save men. Present-day preaching does not even annoy men, but leaves them precisely where they were, without a ruffle and without the slightest disturbance. Anyone who happens to break these rules and who produces a disturbing effect upon members of his congregation is regarded as an objectionable person.[21]

All over America there are preachers who are against sin in their hearts, but are afraid to say so behind their pulpits. They fear the lost people in their congregations. They may preach with loud voices (although this is rapidly becoming a thing of the past), but they do not preach against the sins in their own congregations. The Bible says, "The fear of man bringeth a snare . . ." (Proverbs 29:25).

Many other preachers are even worse: they are actually false prophets. Jesus said, "Many false prophets shall rise, and shall deceive many" (Matthew 24:11). Few thinking people would question the fact that many of the preachers in our day are false prophets. God said: "I have not sent these prophets, yet they ran: I have not spoken to them, yet they prophesied" (Jeremiah 23:21).

Like the false prophets of Jeremiah's day, these modern preachers are "boneless wonders."

Oh, that God would raise up men to preach converting messages to this generation! Oh, for God to raise up men like Edwards, Nettleton, and Spurgeon, to confront our people with the saving message! Oh, for preaching like that in olden times!

Read Old Books to See the Change

Brian H. Edwards writes, "The problem is that we have forgotten what God has done in the past, or we are not particularly interested in being reminded. Mention church history and Christians scatter."[22] Yet it is only by knowing what happened historically that we can correctly evaluate what is happening now.

Alvin Toffler, in his book, *Future Shock*, describes modern people who are "so ignorant of the past that they see nothing unusual about the present."[23] Most books and articles on Christian history today are written by those who see revivals through the "glasses" of a decisionist view of conversion. The best way to understand what evangelicals believed in the past is *not* to read these current books, but to study those that were written in the time-period of the great revivals themselves. They are called "primary sources." To comprehend the great shift that has taken place in evangelical thought regarding conversion, one has to read what was written in the past regarding this subject. Then one can see how much change has occurred through Finney's decisionist methodology.

A Treatise on Conversion was written by the Rev. Richard Baxter in 1657. It was republished countless times, and was one of the main textbooks influencing the ideas of many preachers, from John Bunyan to Jonathan Edwards to George Whitefield. This book had a direct influence on all three of America's Great Awakenings. Its contents characterize what the average evangelical believed in that day. I am quoting from an edition published by the American Tract Society in 1830, before Finney's ideas of decisionism changed the way people see salvation. In the prefatory notice, at the beginning of the American Tract Society edition of Baxter's book, the editor allows that "a few pages, chiefly of more abstract discussion on points which have now lost their interest or on which evangelical Christians differ, have been omitted."[24] This quote shows that Baxter's main ideas on conversion were accepted by virtually all mainstream evangelicals before Finney introduced his methods.

Now, here are the tests that Baxter gave for determining whether a person is converted or not:

I shall here tell you for the negative, who they are who are yet unconverted, and must be changed, if ever they will be saved.

(1) *They who never yet perceived and felt that sin is a great and detestable evil, deserving the wrath of God, and who never*

felt their need of the pardon of sin by the blood of the Lord Jesus, nor were ever humbled because of their rebellion against God, *are yet unconverted,* and without conversion cannot be saved. Matt. 11:28; Luke 13:3,5; Psa. 51:17; Isa. 57:15; Luke 14:11; 18:14.

(2) *That man who was never led to Christ for deliverance, nor beaten out of the conceit of merit or sufficiency in himself,* nor brought to admire the glorious design of God in the great work of redemption, nor to relish the sweetness of the glad tidings of salvation brought to distressed sinners in the gospel, so that his heart was never warmed with the sense of the Redeemer's love, but who hears and reads the gospel as a common story, or as if it were not he who was thus redeemed, *is yet unconverted,* whatever he may seem or think. Phil. 3:8–9; Eph. 3:18–19; Luke 7:47–48; Rom. 10:15; Acts 13:32.

(3) *That person who has not had his heart and hopes in heaven, and looks not at that as his only happiness, and does not make it the business of his life to attain it, but sets his heart more on the things of this life, is certainly unconverted,* whatever he may pretend. Phil. 3:20; Matt. 6:21; Rom. 5:2; Titus 1:2; Heb. 11; 1 Cor. 15:19; Col. 1:5, 23.

(4) *That person who is not weary of all known sin, and hates it not; who would not be rid of it with all his heart,* and is not willing to be at the labor or cost of duty, in the use of those means which God has required for obtaining this conquest, but will venture his soul on a careless life rather than be brought to diligent godliness, and takes up godliness on mere necessity; who would rather let it alone if he dared, and takes it as a grievous thing to be hindered from his sin, *that person is not as yet converted,* but must have a further change before he can be brought into a state of life. Luke 18:23–24; Rom. 6:14,16–7, 21; 7:13,22,24; Psa. 119:5.

(5) *That person who does not heartily engage in the duties of holiness to God, and righteousness and mercy toward man;* who has not the Spirit of Christ within him, and the image of God

upon him, *and does not express it in his worship and obedience,* and is not compassionate and merciful to others, nor humble in his own eyes, nor delights in doing good, nor is willing to do as he would be done by, I say *that person is not truly converted,* whatever appearances of conversion he may have, but must yet be converted or be condemned. Matt. 5:20; Heb. 12:14; 1 Peter 1:15, 16; 2:5; 2 Peter 3:11; Heb. 3:1; Psa. 1:2.

Alas, what multitudes of sinners are yet in the state of death. And how little do they believe it, or lay it to heart . . . it must be, therefore, *that they think they are converted when they are not;* and that is the thing which deceives them and quiets them in their misery.[25]

How many today could pass Baxter's tests for conversion, printed for use by mainstream evangelicals in the early nineteenth century? Surely a remnant could pass, but I fear that this remnant is quite small.

How many have "perceived and felt that sin is a great and detestable evil, deserving the wrath of God"? How many have "conceit of merit or sufficiency in [themselves] beaten out"? How many have their "heart and hopes in heaven"? How many are "weary of all known sin"? How many "heartily engage in the duties of holiness to God" (eager church attendance, daily Bible reading, daily prayer, etc.)? Most evangelicals today would think that a person couldn't pass Baxter's tests without being a strong disciple for several years, perhaps a missionary or elderly pastor. *But Baxter gives these to test whether one is born again or not!* And you will note that this was the opinion of mainstream evangelicals before Finney. It was the general thought on conversion prior to the beginning of "decisionism" as we know it today.

No wonder the old time converts became wonderful Christians, while those who claim to be born again today often miss church, live loose lives, and hold false doctrines. The simple difference is this: large numbers of people who have made a decision today are going to Hell. Baxter was right. They are not converted.

One point cannot be refuted: Baxter's beliefs were held by mainstream evangelicals, as the American Tract Society pointed out in the preface to the edition published in 1830. Finney's ideas had not yet produced the decisionism which has now engulfed us, and added millions of lost people to our churches.

Pilgrim's Progress Shows How Modern Evangelism Changed
John Bunyan (1628–1688) is undoubtedly the most widely read Baptist of all time. The only book in English which has passed his *Pilgrim's Progress* in sales is the *King James Bible*. Bunyan's book is considered the finest allegory ever written. An allegory is not fiction, but a story which uses symbols or images to represent something which is true. In *Pilgrim's Progress* Bunyan pictures a man going through his life on earth as a journey. This character, named Christian, passes through various trials and difficulties as he travels from the City of Destruction, through the world, on his way to the Celestial City.

The story begins with Christian crying out, "What must I do to be saved?" He awakes the next morning filled with great heaviness of mind. He walks about the fields in distress. At last he meets a man named Evangelist who tells him, "Fly from the wrath to come." He asks, "Which way must I fly?" Evangelist says, "Do you see that narrow [Wicket] gate?" Christian says, "No." "Do you see that light?" He then says, "I think I do." "Keep that light in your eye," says Evangelist, "and go straight up to it; so shall you see the gate, at which when you knock, it shall be told you what you are to do."

Christian leaves the City of Destruction to find the narrow gate so he can enter through it and be saved. Notice that Evangelist does not have this man say a sinner's prayer, learn the plan of salvation, or make a Lordship commitment. Instead, the Evangelist points him to Jesus, Himself.

Christian is now off on his search for Jesus. He carries a great load on his back, which symbolizes the weight of sin. His wife and children try to stop him as he leaves home to find Jesus. They give a loud wail and beg him to come back to the City of Destruction, but he runs away crying, "Life! Life!" Friends of his wife come after him and try to persuade him to turn back with them to the city. One of them is named Obstinate. He scoffs at Christian's search for Christ. His companion, named Pliable, says that if the joys and blessings Christian speaks of are true, they appear to be worth searching for. Obstinate cries, "What! More fools, still! Go back, go back, and be wise." When Pliable joins Christian in his search for Jesus, Obstinate declares, "I will go back to my place; I will not be one of such vain folks."

Christian and Pliable go off on their search for Jesus. Soon the road they are travelling goes through a slough (*sloo*, a swampy marsh). Here they lay for some time, stuck in the mud, and sinking more and more in the mire. Pliable says this wallowing in mire has not brought him the happiness Christian spoke about, so he leaves Christian in the mud and goes back to the City of Destruction.

Wallowing in the slough, Christian is at last greeted by a man named Help, who tells him what the muddy marsh means. "When a man wakes up to a sense of his own lost state, doubts and fears rise up in his soul, and all of them drain down and sink into this place." He then tells Christian how to get out of the mire and return to his search for Christ.

Next Christian meets Worldly Wiseman, a person only interested in earthly pleasures. This man gives worldly advice to Christian. He tells him, "I have seen more of the world than you. In the way you go, you will meet with pain. Pay no attention to what Evangelist tells you." Then Worldly Wiseman tells him to go to a town called Morality and speak to a man named Legality and his son, Civility, and they will tell him how to get the load of sin off of his back without going through the narrow gate (i.e. without coming to Christ). So Christian goes out of the way to find Mr. Legality's house to seek help in removing his heavy burden. He meets Evangelist on the way. Evangelist says, "What doest thou here, Christian?" Christian cannot answer. Evangelist goes on,

"Art not thou the man that I heard cry in the City of Destruction?"

Christian: "Yes, dear sir, I am that man."

Evangelist: "Did not I point out to thee the way to the Narrow Gate?" (Christ).

Christian: "Yes, you did, Sir."

Evangelist: "How is it, then, that thou hast so soon gone out of the way?"

Christian: "When I had got out the Slough of Despond I met a man who told me that in a town near, I might find one who could take off my load. He got me at last to yield; so I came here."

When Evangelist had heard from Christian all that took place, he said, "The just shall live by faith, but if a man draw back, my soul shall have no joy in him. Is not this the case with thee? Hast not thou drawn back thy feet from the way of peace? Give more heed to the things that I shall tell thee of. The Lord says, 'Strive to go in at the strait gate to which I send thee, for strait is the gate that leads to life, and few there be that find it.' Why didst thou disregard the Word of God and listen to Mr. Worldly Wiseman? The man whom he sent thee to, Legality, could not set thee free; no man has got rid of his load through him; he could only show thee the way to woe, for by the deeds of the law no man can get rid of his load."

Christian to Evangelist: "Sir, what do you think? Is there hope? May I now go back, and strive to reach the Narrow Gate?"

Evangelist: "Thy sin is great, for thou hast gone from the way that is good, to tread false paths, yet will the man at the gate let thee through, for he has love and good will for all men. But be careful that thou turn not to the right hand or to the left."

So he went on in haste, and could by no means feel safe till he was in the path which he had left. In time he got up to the gate. He gave three knocks and said, "May I go in here?"

The gatekeeper said, "Who is there? Where did you come from, and what do you want?"

Christian: "I come from the City of Destruction with a load of sins on my back; but I am on my way to Mount Zion, that I might be free from the wrath to come; and as I have been told that my way is through this gate, I would know, Sir, if you will let me in."

The gatekeeper then flung back the gate as Christian went in. He then ran till he drew near to a place on which stood a cross, and at the foot of it a tomb. Just as Christian came up to the cross, his load slid from his back. Then Christian was glad, and said, "He gives me rest by his grief, and life by his death."

The Great Baptist Author Speaks on Conversion

This sketch of "Christian's" conversion has been simplified and reduced to a bare outline of what Bunyan gave in *Pilgrim's Progress*. Originally "Christian's" conversion experience covers about one-fourth of the book. It has been outlined here to show how the idea of conversion has been changed to mere decisionism in evangelical thought today.

If a lost person were trying to leave the City of Destruction and find relief from his burden of sin, what evangelical evangelist in our time would advise him the way Evangelist did in *Pilgrim's Progress*? Few, if any, I fear, would point such a man to Jesus, Himself, who is the narrow gate to eternal life. Few, if any, evangelical evangelists would continue to point a man to Jesus, though the man's family and friends pulled him back, though he went astray in a period of depression and hopelessness (the slough), though he were given false advice by the lost. Who, through all these events, would continue to point a lost man to Jesus? The vast majority of evangelical evangelists today would just have him say a quick prayer, or learn a couple of verses, or make a Lordship commitment.

Pilgrim's Progress shows us that today's "conversions" are quite different from those in the time of John Bunyan, in the seventeenth century. Read this classic again and ask yourself if you have anyone in your church with a testimony like "Christian's", or *if you have ever even met anyone with such a testimony*. Think over the fact that testimonies like this were common in the seventeenth, eighteenth, and early nineteenth centuries. Then ask yourself, *what caused this change if it wasn't Finney's decisionism?*

One ought to remember that *Pilgrim's Progress* consistently out-sold all books but the Bible for two hundred years. It was read and loved by Wesleyans as well as Calvinists. All branches of evangelicalism embraced it as a correct explanation of Christian conversion. Why? Because salvation experiences like this were quite common before Finney changed conversion into decisionism.

What evangelical evangelist today would give the kind of advice, over a considerable period of time, that the evangelist gave in *Pilgrim's Progress?* The evangelists of our day have largely turned away from the old paths. As a result, almost no one today has a conversion similar to Christian's.

While we do not think that every convert must go through an extended period of doubt and uncertainty, we can know for sure, by the long popularity of Bunyan's book, that this was quite often the case before Finney changed the meaning of conversion. Today, evangelical evangelists would pray instantly with the man in the story, or tell him that he had already been saved. Today, the average evangelical evangelist would demand a decision right then, on the spot, regardless of the man's spiritual state. He would then give the man some false assurance, and leave him unconverted, awaiting Hell.

Thus, by reading Richard Baxter's *Treatise on Conversion* and John Bunyan's *Pilgrim's Progress*, one can see how conversion was changed into a mere decision by Finney and his followers in the mid-nineteenth century.

Church Splits—a Result of Decisionism

Decisionism not only deludes people into thinking they are saved, but it also has brought ruin and confusion to the churches. Religious News Service reports, in a national survey of Protestant clergy, that 22.8 percent of the pastors say they have been fired at some point during their career.[27] David L. Goetz, the associate editor of *Leadership,* who conducted the survey, said, "Denominational leaders often stand by and watch a percentage of their churches destroy pastor after pastor."[28] This survey shows that about one out of every four pastors has been fired.

According to another survey, "ninety-nine percent of all pastors reported severe division of one sort or another during their ministries."[29] This survey also shows that eighty-nine percent of independent Baptists have experienced at least "one outright split."[30]

These two surveys reveal that one out of four pastors has been fired, and virtually every other pastor has experienced "severe division" during his ministry. This is another result of adding people to the churches by decisions instead of conversions.

Unconverted church members cause severe division. Unconverted church members fire pastors. As the old saying goes, "You pay now or you pay later." If you add people who are unconverted to the church now, you will pay for it later. Most pastors have paid many times over for baptizing or transferring into their churches people who are unconverted.

Think of the untold horror that people experience through church splits. Think of the shattered lives, broken relationships, and destroyed hopes that have been caused by church fights. Some of the most vicious actions I have ever seen or heard of have occurred through church splits.

Having lived through one church split as a teenager, one when I was in my twenties, and several since then, I can say without hesitation that church splits do more harm to the cause of Christ than any other single problem in the churches. Roy Branson writes, "Church split! The two most dreaded words to a preacher. Each hopes it will never come to him. In his early ministry he dares believe it will not, cannot happen to him. But it does!"[31]

I have become convinced, through my own observation of church splits, that the main cause of them is unconverted church members. A classic division, given as a type of church splits, illustrates this. Moses, as the leader of the congregation (similar to a New Testament pastor), experienced rebellion against his authority by the "church splitter" and his crowd (Numbers 16:3). In the following verses, the split grew. The end of the account has the leader of the division falling into the open pit of Hell (Numbers 16:33).

We read about the fulfillment of this type in the New Testament. Here, in the antitype,* it is quite clear that God is speaking about church splits:

> But these speak evil of those things which they know not: but what they know naturally, as brute beasts, in those things they corrupt themselves. Woe unto them! for they have gone in the way of Cain, and ran greedily after the error of Balaam for reward, and perished in the gainsaying of Core. These are spots in your feasts of charity, when they feast with you, feeding themselves without fear: clouds they are without water, carried about of winds; trees whose fruit withereth, without fruit, twice dead, plucked up by the roots; Raging waves of the sea, foaming out their own shame; wandering stars, to whom is reserved the blackness of darkness for ever.
>
> —Jude 10–13

The Scofield note on the eighth verse of Jude is somewhat confusing. It says, "Apostate teachers described." This seems to imply that theological "teachers" in apostate seminaries or colleges are the people being described. But the Bible does not speak in Jude of "teachers" in theological seminaries or colleges. There were no theological seminaries or colleges, and no such teachers, when the Epistle of Jude was written. **_The passage does not speak of "teachers" at all._** Instead, the verse is simply speaking of those who cause rebellion and "despise dominion" (verse 8) in the local church. We are told that they will perish in gainsaying (or speaking against) like Korah did. In other words, they will speak against authority, often the authority of the pastor, as Korah spoke against Moses in Numbers 16. Then, in verse 12, we are told that they attend the Lord's Supper, the "feasts of charity." Finally, we are told that these rebellious people will be sent to Hell, to the "black-

---

* A type is an Old Testament illustration, given in advance. An antitype is the New Testament fulfillment of the type.

ness of darkness" (see verse 13). That is a clear indication that these railers and church splitters are unconverted people, especially the ones who lead a split. These lost people have "crept in unawares," into the membership of the local church (Jude 4).

In 1 Corinthians 6:10, "revilers" are listed with homosexuals, drunkards, fornicators, and thieves. The word "reviler" means "one who speaks with abusive, railing backtalk." This is a person who leads church splits. We are plainly told that they shall not ". . . inherit the kingdom of God . . ." (1 Corinthians 6:10). So, the Bible tells us that those who lead church splits, who rail, who lead rebellions like Korah, are not converted, but are unsaved people who have come into the church but have never known true salvation.

Notice that nearly every person who leads a church split has made a decision at some time in his life. All of those who perished in the gainsaying of Korah had done so. They had made a decision to leave Egypt. They had made a decision to follow Moses. And virtually all of those who will not inherit the kingdom of God because of their "reviling" have at some time in the past made a "decision." But a decision like this does not stop such a man from attacking his pastor, confusing the young people in the Sunday school, and destroying the church.

Crows Are the Mockingbird's Natural Enemy

I well remember one deacon who worked with all of his might to get a pastor fired so that he could take the money out of a bank account and keep it for himself. The pastor of that church called me several times each week asking for prayer and counsel. It was a heartbreaking thing to behold. This pastor agreed with me that the deacon could not be a saved person, but was like Judas, who was a thief (cf. John 12:6). Yet the deacon had made a decision years before.

In another church, a sex pervert led the choir. He split the church wide open by taking little children to bed with him and having sex with them. People fled with horror from the church. Families were broken. People were confused. The man who caused all of this had made a decision in a leading Southern Baptist church, but had not been converted. Like the deacon who was a thief, he had raised his hand, gone forward, or said a sinner's prayer, but had not received a new nature, had not been born again.

I have lived in Southern California for nearly sixty years. In the memories of my childhood, it was beautiful almost beyond description. Now many ugly things crowd out the beauty. When I was a boy, the California mockingbird was everywhere. It sings at night, you know. The lovely warble of this gentle bird once punctuated warm California evenings with heart-lifting music. Now we seldom hear them. They are being crowded out by the crows. You see, the crows are the mockingbird's natural enemy. Crows raid their nests, break their eggs, and eat their young.

Great clouds of these crows now blacken the skies in many parts of Southern California. I have read several articles on this phenomenon recently. It seems that restrictions on firearms have removed man as a player in this drama. We no longer shoot the crows, so their population has exploded. The mockingbirds don't have a chance.

That's similar to what has happened in our churches. The crows are multiplying and the mockingbirds are disappearing. When religious-but-lost people pack our churches, it makes a very dangerous environment for our children, and a hostile, unfriendly one for every real Christian.

It is dismal to see the sky blackened with crows. It is sad to occasionally see one lone mockingbird trying to hold on. That's the situation in many evangelical churches today.

Chaos on Sunday Morning

Once I saw the pastor of a large church in the Southern Baptist Convention sitting with tears running down his face, his head in his hands, rocking back and forth and sobbing, while seated in the pastor's chair behind the pulpit. Before him, hundreds of people cursed one another with foul language, and some even threw hymnbooks across the aisles at each other. People cursed one another. Three men grabbed a church leader and threw him on the sidewalk in front of the church, taking him by the throat, and beating his head against the pavement. When he was unconscious, they rifled his pockets and took away his key to the church building.

This was done at 11:00 a.m. on a Sunday morning, during the morning worship service. I saw it with my own eyes as a seventeen-year-old boy. All of these people had made "decisions." All of them had said a sinner's prayer, gone forward, or lifted their hand. But how many of them could have been converted? Even then it seemed impossible to me that real Christians could behave in such an utterly indecent fashion in the house of God, if they had anything in the way of the new birth (cf. John 3:7).

Now, it is true that carnal Christians may take part in such splits. First Corinthians 3:1–4 seems to indicate that divisions can be led by carnal people. The word "carnal" is used. However, in Galatians 5:20 the same Greek word (*dichostasia*) is used which we find in 1 Corinthians 3:3. The passage in Galatians plainly tells us "that they which do such things shall not inherit the kingdom of God" (Galatians 5:19–21). From a study of these two passages, I believe we can determine this: Most church splits are caused by carnal Christians and lost people pretending to be Christians. Such splits are usually led by lost people (Galatians 5:19–21). Carnal Christians often follow these lost people in such a division (1 Corinthians 3:1–3). No decent convert will ever participate in a church split.

It seems significant to me that the word "seditions" in Galatians 5:20 is *dichostasia* and means "one who causes divisions." This same Greek word is used in Romans 16:17, where Christians are told to keep their eyes open for those who cause divisions. These people are to be avoided according to this verse. Thus, the New Testament shows us the evil of church splits, and in Galatians 5:19–21 and Jude 11–13, the Bible shows us that most leaders of church splits are lost people. Yet, in the twentieth century, virtually all these lost leaders have "made decisions."

Wouldn't Korah be a member of an evangelical church today? Wouldn't most Baptist churches accept his membership on the basis of his decision? After all, Korah had made a decision to leave Egypt. He had made a decision to pass through the Red Sea. He had made a decision to eat the Passover. He was an upstanding man in the congregation. Yet the Bible tells us the ground opened up and he fell alive into the flames of Hell. And the New Testament uses him in the book of Jude (Jude 11–13) as an illustration of people going to Hell. Korah is a clear example of a person who makes a decision, but is not converted. Anyone in a local church who remains in an unconverted state, as Korah did, will be lost for eternity. Even upstanding leaders in the church who have made decisions will go to Hell without a conversion.

Judas Made a Decision

In the New Testament, Judas is a clear example of someone who has made a decision without being converted. We are plainly told that Jesus chose twelve apostles and that one of them was Judas (cf. Luke 6:12–16). In Matthew 10 we are told that He "called unto him his twelve disciples." The verse goes on to say that He gave them power in prayer, in connection with demons, sickness, and other matters. Then we are told that Judas Iscariot, ". . . who also betrayed him, . . ." was one of these men that He called (cf. Matthew 10:1–4). Now, this shows that Judas was a man who was called by Jesus. It shows that he made a decision to follow Christ. It also shows us that he had prayers answered,* including miracles, given in answer to his prayers. Yet, we are told later that he went to Hell (cf. Acts 1:25).

Judas was the treasurer among the twelve apostles (John 12:6).

---

* The idea that God *never* answers the prayers of a lost person was expressed by a man who was still lost himself (John 9:31). This man was not converted until later (John 9:38). A clear example of God answering the prayers of a lost man is given in Acts 10:4, 31. Judas also had many prayers answered even though he remained unconverted.

Isn't it possible that some church treasurers today are also unconverted? How many deacons? How many choir directors? How many members of the choir? How many Sunday school teachers? How many pastors? How many pastor's wives? How many evangelists? Since one of the original twelve in the first church was an unconverted man, many church members today could also be unconverted, couldn't they?

Judas would gladly have raised his hand in an evangelistic meeting. He would gladly have gone forward at a "decision time." In fact, we are plainly told that Judas made a decision and went forth as a sheep in the midst of wolves (Matthew 10:16). He willingly went and witnessed for Christ, though he himself was lost. He clearly made a decision to follow Christ. "And he called unto him the twelve, and began to send them forth two by two" (Mark 6:7). So, Judas had many prayers answered, went soulwinning, appeared to be clean living, and had made his decision to follow Christ. But the devil came and possessed him because he was unconverted. The Bible says that "Satan entered into him" (John 13:27; cf. John 6:70–71). Judas became possessed by Satan because he was an unconverted man. He had been religious, but he was lost. He was like so many thousands in our churches today.

I think it is self-evident that Korah and Judas are types of those who lead church splits. Notice that the Bible says that Judas ". . . went immediately out . . ." (John 13:30). This is surely a picture of leaving the local church. His further actions resulted in the scattering of the disciples: ". . . Then all the disciples forsook him, and fled . . ." (Matthew 26:56). Many are scattered today through the actions of men like Judas.

Thus, in the Old and New Testaments, we have these two pictures of lost people causing dreadful splits, confusion, and turmoil. How many are just like Korah or Judas today? How many have made decisions without being converted?

They went out from us, but they were not of us; for if they had been of us, they would no doubt have continued with us: but they went out, that they might be made manifest that they were not all of us.

—I John 2:19

Although we disagree with John MacArthur on several subjects, we are in agreement with his comments on 1 John 2:19, given in *The MacArthur Study Bible:*

> The first characteristic mentioned of antichrists, i.e. false teachers and deceivers, is that they depart from the faithful. *They arise from within the church and depart from true fellowship and lead people out with them.* The verse also places emphasis on the perseverance of the saints. . . . *Those genuinely born again endure in faith and fellowship and the truth.* The ultimate test of true Christianity is endurance. *The departure of people from the truth and the church is their unmasking.*[32]

On this point, Dr. MacArthur is correct and biblical. His statement on 1 John 2:19 says that deceivers cause church splits because they are not genuinely converted. They leave the church and "depart from the faithful" because they have never been "genuinely born again."

A wise pastor should see that unconverted people have given him trouble for years. His own best interest is served by making sure that his people have been converted, rather than merely making decisions.

Footnotes

1. John R. Rice, *The Sword of the Lord,* September 19, 1997.
2. Brian H. Edwards, *Revival! A People Saturated With God* (Durham, England: Evangelical Press, 1991), p. 218.
3. Ibid, p. 219.
4. Ibid
5. Ibid., p. 220.
6. Ibid., pp. 220–221.
7. C. H. Spurgeon, *Lectures to My Students* (Pasadena, TX: Pilgrim Publications, 1990), pp. 23–24.

8. Dr. E. C. Carrier in *Dear Preacher, Please Quit* by Roy L. Branson, Jr. (Lancaster, CA: Landmark Publications, 1987), p. 25.

9. Ibid., p. 26.

10. Ibid., p. 29.

11. Nettleton, *Sermons from the Second Great Awakening,* pp. 162–63.

12. Matthew Poole, *A Commentary on the Holy Bible* (Edinburgh: Banner of Truth Trust, 1990 edition, first edition 1685), vol. 3, pp. 637–38.

13. Jonathan Edwards, *The Works of Jonathan Edwards, Volume Two* (Edinburgh: The Banner of Truth Trust; 1992, from the 1834 edition), p. 174.

14. Albert Barnes, *Notes on the New Testament,* 1 Corinthians (Grand Rapids, MI: Baker Book House, 1983, reprinted from the 1885 edition by Blackie and Son, London), p. 268.

15. C. H. Spurgeon, *The New Park Street Pulpit, Volume IV* (Pasadena, TX: Pilgrim Publications, 1981 reprint), p. 429.

16. C. H. Spurgeon, *Metropolitan Tabernacle Pulpit, Volume 30* (Pasadena, TX: Pilgrim Publications, 1973 reprint), p. 371.

17. J. Vernon McGee, *Thru the Bible* (Nashville: Thomas Nelson, 1983), vol. 5, p. 145.

18. Asahel Nettleton, *Sermons From the Second Great Awakening,* pp. 323, 333.

19. Winston S. Churchill speech recorded by Martin Gilbert, *Prophet of Truth* (London: Mandarin paperbacks, 1990), p. 389.

20. J. Gresham Machen, *Christianity and Liberalism* (Grand Rapids, MI: Wm. B. Eerdmans, reprinted 1983), p. 68.

21. Quoted by Iain H. Murray, *David Martyn Lloyd-Jones: The First Forty Years 1899–1939* (Edinburgh: Banner of Truth Trust, 1983), p. 206.

22. Brian H. Edwards, *Revival! A People Saturated With God* (Durham, England: Evangelical Press, 1991), p.87.

23. Alvin Toffler, *Future Shock* (New York: Bantam Books, 1971), p. 20.

24. In *A Treatise on Conversion* by Richard Baxter (New York: American Tract Society, 1830 edition), preparatory notice.

25. Richard Baxter, *A Treatise on Conversion* (New York: American Tract Society, 1830), pp. 193–95.

26. John Bunyan, *Pilgrim's Progress,* adapted from a simplified version in *Of People,* edited by Ian Anderson (Pensacola, FL: A Beka Book Publications, 1995), pp. 144–54.

27. Los Angeles *Times,* January 6, 1996, p. B-11.

28. Ibid.

29. Roy Branson, Jr., *Church Split* (Bristol, TN: Landmark Publications, 1990), p. 267.

30. Ibid.

31. Ibid., p. 3.

32. John MacArthur, *The MacArthur Study Bible* (Nashville: Word Publishing, 1997), note on 1 John 2:19.

Chapter Five

A False Prophet

And many false prophets shall rise, and shall deceive many . . .
>—Matthew 24:11

The atonement did not consist in the literal payment of the debt of sinners.
>—Charles G. Finney

For sinners to be forensically [legally] pronounced just, is impossible and absurd.
>—Charles G. Finney

Christ could not have died for anyone else's sins than his own.
>—Charles G. Finney paraphrased by Dr. Michael S. Horton

This system is in many ways of its elements simply a reproduction of the Romish errors against which our fathers bore testimony in the days of the Reformation.
>—H. E. Jacobs, nineteenth century author

We have shown in several ways how decisionism has harmed evangelical Christianity and filled our churches with lost people. We have shown how unconverted church members cause church splits and do great harm to the work of Christ. We believe that decisionism has also stopped revival, so that a real revival is very rare today. But where did decisionism come from? Where did the idea of making a decision instead of being converted begin?

We have become convinced that Charles G. Finney started this trend. After studying the subject for several years, we think that the finger of guilt is pointed directly at Finney.

When you talk about Finney, many good people may think that you are speaking against revival. This is largely due to the impression, which has been almost universal since 1900, that Finney actually *introduced* revivals in the nineteenth century.[1] Finney's *Memoirs* helped to promote this idea. But these memoirs were written long after the events, and were published to prove his theories concerning decisionism.[2] The memoirs have been in print ever since the first edition in 1876. The influence of this book has been so great that it has led many people to think that Finney brought revival to America. This belief has been repeated so often that many people regard it as a fact. For instance, Billy Graham wrote of Finney: "Through his Spirit-filled ministry, uncounted thousands came to know Christ in the nineteenth century, resulting in one of the greatest periods of revival in the history of America."[3]

When the facts are examined, however, they reveal that Dr. Graham's statement is faulty. Finney began preaching toward the end of the Second Great Awakening. America had been through its greatest revival in the First Great Awakening (1734–1740) and most of the Second Great Awakening (1800–1830). Finney's most important years were 1821 to 1829. So we see that Dr. Graham's evaluation is not true to the facts. The First Great Awakening occurred nearly a hundred years before Finney appeared on the scene. The Second Great Awakening had already been going on for twenty-one years. Finney only held a prominent place in the last ten years. He held no important leadership position in the Third Great Awakening, beginning in 1858. By that time he was an elderly man whose ministry was largely confined to the presidency of Oberlin College. Also, Finney's techniques were not used at all in the introduction or carrying out of the 1858 awakening. This revival was the product of prayer, without the use of the methods he gave in *Revival Lectures* and elsewhere.[4]

Vernon J. Charlesworth, who was the head of Spurgeon's orphanage, wrote this in the May 1876 edition of Spurgeon's paper, *The Sword and the Trowel*: "We gravely question whether the supposed benefit of Mr. Finney's labours has not been greatly overestimated. Discount, very large discount, must be made, ere the truth is reached."[5]

A careful study of history reveals that Charles G. Finney did *not* introduce revival to America in any sense, and that his methods have not been used to *produce* revival in any notable way. In fact, no national or regional revival has occurred since Finney's ideas became prominent, except for the 1905 Welsh revival and the 1949 Isle of Lewis revival. Mr. Finney's methods were not conspicuous in either of these awakenings.

Finney has been a great promoter of his own methods of decisionism, however. He has become the best known preacher from the past century through his own self-aggrandizing writings. In fact, Finney was so successful in promoting himself that he alone is remembered by most people when they think of the revivals in the nineteenth century. Many people, however, do not look carefully at what Finney believed and taught. And most do not see how Finney's ideas changed mainstream evangelicalism from seeking conversions to promoting decisions, and most have not seen how his ideas harm us and have brought about the apostasy of our time.

Christ gave us a simple test for discerning the difference between false prophets and true prophets:

> Beware of false prophets, which come to you in sheep's clothing, but inwardly they are ravening wolves. Ye shall know them by their fruits. Do men gather grapes of thorns, or figs of thistles? Even so every good tree bringeth forth good fruit; but a corrupt tree bringeth forth evil fruit. A good tree cannot bring forth evil fruit, neither can a corrupt tree bring forth good fruit. Every tree that bringeth not forth good fruit is hewn down, and cast into the fire. Wherefore by their fruits ye shall know them.
>
> —Matthew 7:15–20

Jesus made these points on false prophets:

1. You can tell false prophets by their fruits (Matthew 7:15–16).
2. ". . . Good trees bring forth good fruit; corrupt trees bring forth evil fruit . . . " (Matthew 7:17–18).
3. Therefore, the test of true and false prophets is the fruits they produce (Matthew 7:20).

According to this test, Charles G. Finney was a false prophet. His ministry brought forth these evil fruits: (1) false doctrine, (2) decisionism which has ruined evangelism, and (3) the movement which is drawing new evangelicals ever closer to reunion with the Catholic Church. There can be no question that Finney is revealed as a false prophet by the test Christ gave us in Matthew 7:15–20.

Finney's False Doctrine

Let us focus on three of Finney's doctrines and show how they have hurt the churches and promoted decisionism:

1. Finney believed that a converted person could lose his salvation.
2. Finney denied the atonement of Christ and the imputation of Christ's righteousness.
3. Finney taught that conversion is based on a choice, not on the work of the Holy Spirit within the soul.

When these views of Finney are laid out in modern English, they are exposed as unscriptural, and seem strange to us. Yet the result of these teachings is the evangelical decisionism so prevalent in the churches around us.

First, Finney believed that a converted person could lose his salvation. He wrote:

If real Christians do backslide, they lose for the time being their evidence of acceptance with God; and withal they know that in their present state they cannot be saved. This objection is leveled rather against that view of perseverance that says, "once in grace, always in grace."[6]

Finney railed against the doctrine of "once saved, always saved," saying there is "no ground of hope to a backslider, except on condition of return and perseverance to the end."[7] Thus, Finney held that a saved person could lose his salvation. He strongly protested against "perpetual justification upon condition of one act of faith."[8] He clearly taught that the new birth does not come through a one-time act of faith in Christ. It is often surprising, when listening to the testimonies of evangelicals, how many of them believe that you can move in and out of salvation. This is largely a result of Finney's ideas filtering down to the common man.

Finney Leads to Rome

Furthermore, Finney taught that salvation can be lost and regained repeatedly. This is not Baptist or Protestant doctrine. It is not Bible doctrine. It is a return to the Roman Catholic doctrine of salvation by good works, confessions, restitutions, and the whole Roman system of self-salvation. A person who talks to Roman Catholics and listens to them will discover that their view of salvation is nearly identical to that of Charles G. Finney. Like Finney, Catholics believe that one act of faith in Jesus does not save. Like Finney, they believe that one can lose and regain his salvation repeatedly. This idea of moving in and out of salvation again and again has become quite common among evangelicals in our time. That is probably the main reason that "rededications" have become so prominent in the last hundred years.

No wonder Finney's "decisionism" has ended with evangelicals in the late twentieth century coming into full cooperation with the Roman Catholic Church. Leading evangelicals and Catholics have issued a major document titled "Evangelicals and Catholics Together." This document was signed by Charles Colson, Bill Bright, Pat Robertson, J. I. Packer, and Roman Catholics like Cardinal

O'Connor, Archbishop Francis Stafford, Father Richard John Neuhaus, and Father Avery Dulles, plus Mark Noll of Wheaton College, Richard Land of the SBC Christian Life Commission, and Larry Lewis of the SBC Home Mission Board. (Lewis and Land later withdrew their signatures after it caused trouble for them, but continued to express strong personal support for the document).

Here are selections from "Evangelicals and Catholics Together":

We together, Evangelicals and Catholics, confess our sins against the unity that Christ intends. . . . The two communities in world Christianity that are the most evangelically assertive are Evangelicals and Catholics. . . . *Evangelicals and Catholics are brothers and sisters in Christ.* . . . However difficult the way, we recognize that we are called by God to a fuller recognition of our unity . . . greater visible unity for which we hope. . . . *Those converted—whether understood as having received the new birth for the first time or as having experienced the reawakening of the new birth originally bestowed in the Sacrament of baptism*—must be given full freedom and respect. . . . It [conversion] is a continuing process.[9]

These brief excerpts from "Evangelicals and Catholics Together" illustrate the great confusion over conversion brought on by Finney's methods—decisionist confusion which is bringing evangelicals into full unity with Rome.

This close cooperation of Roman Catholics with "decisionist" Protestants *is an on-going phenomenon. It is illustrated, for instance, in the Sacramento, California, Billy Graham Crusade of 1995, in which 303 Protestant and 38 Roman Catholic churches worked together for five days. Henry G. Wells, senior pastor of Fair Oaks Presbyterian Church, said, "There is a renewed openness among Catholics. . . . We've had quite a few Catholic counselors who know the Lord."*[10]

If a Roman Catholic truly "knows the Lord," *he is no longer a*

Roman Catholic, for the Roman Catholic Church teaches salvation by a series of decisions, rather than salvation by a one-time trust in Jesus. But it should not surprise us that an evangelical like Dr. Wells thinks that these Catholics are saved. This is a result of Finney's decisionism, where Protestants move in and out of salvation like Roman Catholics did before the Reformation. Finney's decisionism is the road back to Rome.

Writing of Finney's methods in the nineteenth century, H. E. Jacobs said:

> *This system [of Finney's decisionist methods] is in many of its elements simply a reproduction of the Romish errors against which our fathers bore testimony in the days of the Reformation.* Wide as is the apparent difference, we find in both the same corruption of the doctrine of justification by faith alone without works, the same ignorance of the depths of natural depravity, the same exaltation of human strength and merit, the same indifference to sound doctrine, and the same substitution of subjective frames of mind and forms of experience for the great objective facts of Christianity, as the grounds of God's favor.[11]

Jacobs was right when he said this in the nineteenth century. Today Finney's decisionism has so permeated evangelicalism that there is little difference between an evangelical and a Catholic. As a result, there is an ever-growing closeness between decisionists and Romanists.

David W. Cloud has a four-volume set of booklets which trace evangelicalism's journey back to Rome. These books are thoroughly documented. They deal with the connection between Catholicism and Billy Graham, Campus Crusade, James Dobson, Chuck Colson, Jerry Falwell, InterVarsity Christian Fellowship, D. James Kennedy, J. I. Packer, Luis Palau, Youth for Christ, the Southern Baptist Convention, and the charismatic movement. Write to Way of Life Literature concerning these four books: 1701 Harns Rd., Oak Harbor, WA 98277.

The Sword of the Lord reports that Promise Keepers is also joining with Roman Catholics. The editor writes: "The Promise Keepers' front office has apparently had in mind from the outset to give Catholics full participation in their program."[12] Promise Keepers seems to be fading now, but it could remain a threat to our churches.

Promise Keepers Drop Reformation Faith

Promise Keepers is an ecumenical men's movement which began in the U.S. It has expanded into Canada, New Zealand, Australia, South Africa, and elsewhere. Millions of men have joined it. In October 1996 the Promise Keepers' statement of faith regarding salvation was changed from "faith alone" to "only through faith."

The Roman Catholic paper, *Our Sunday Visitor,* reported that this change was made by Promise Keepers to accommodate Roman Catholics who wanted to join but couldn't, "because to embrace 'faith alone' would force them to reject their Catholic faith."[13]

Rev. Robert Looper, a pastor in St. Louis, writes:

> Now according to PK, it is not faith alone in Christ that saves; it is faith in Christ alone that saves. The latter is the classic teaching of the Roman Catholic Church, that faith is a necessary but insufficient condition of salvation; trust in Christ merely begins the process of salvation, which is "completed" as Christ enables us by grace to participate in works of righteousness.[14]

Rev. Looper goes on to say that this may sound like nit-picking today, but it is the very doctrine which led Martin Luther to choose a life of conflict rather than accommodation; it was the very doctrinal distinction which brought about the Reformation. This is another instance of evangelicalism giving up its Protestant and Baptist distinctives and moving toward Rome, as a direct result of the decisionist principles inculcated from the Finney movement in the nineteenth century.

Decisionism at first blurred and finally removed the important distinctions between Catholics and Protestants through a return to Rome-like doctrines of salvation by saying sinner's prayers, rededications, confessions of sin, restitutions, and the whole Romish system of self-salvation. That is why new evangelicalism is going back to Rome today. It is a direct result of Finney's methods and ideas.

You Can Fall Out of Heaven!

Finney was so extreme in his belief that a Christian can lose his salvation that he actually said a Christian could fall out of Heaven and lose it after he dies! Here is the exact quote: "Saints in heaven can by natural possibility apostatize and fall, and be lost. Were not this naturally possible, there would be no virtue in perseverance."[15] Yes, you really read that! Finney actually said that saints in Heaven can fall and be lost! He actually taught that people could fall out of Heaven into Hell!

This idea is a return to the beliefs of the early Catholic theologian Origen. Roman Catholics do not believe this today, however. Thus, Finney was worse than a modern Roman Catholic in his belief that man saves himself by a series of decisions. At least modern Roman Catholics say that once a man gets to Heaven he can't fall out!

This means that Finney believed a man is saved by repeated acts of rededication—even after he gets to Heaven! It means that he rejected salvation as a one-time experience.

The Reformation Rejected

Finney also denied the blood atonement and imputation of Christ's righteousness. He wrote:

> The atonement did not consist in the literal payment of the debt of sinners. It was not true that Christ suffered just what those for whom He died deserved to suffer . . . not that which cancelled sin in the sense of literally paying the indebtedness of sinners.[16]

Finney believed in what is called the governmental theory of atonement, which holds that Christ died "simply to remove an insurmountable obstacle out of the way of God's forgiveness of sinners."[17] *Finney did not believe that Christ died to pay for our sins*. Read the last indented quotation (footnote 16) again carefully and you will see that this is true.

Here are several quotations from Finney which prove that he did not believe that Christ died to pay the debt for our sins:

> Justification is not found in Christ's literally suffering the exact penalty of the law for them [sinners], and in this sense literally purchasing their justification and eternal salvation.[18] . . . You cannot find in your heart to demand "exact justice" at the hand of God, on the ground that Christ has literally paid your debt.[19] . . . For sinners to be forensically [legally] pronounced just, is impossible and absurd.[20]

Michael S. Horton is correct when he paraphrases Finney's view: "Christ could not have died for anyone else's sins than his own."[21]

Remember that Finney said: "The atonement did not consist in the literal payment of the debt of sinners . . . which cancelled sin in the sense of literally paying the indebtedness of sinners."[22]

Finney makes statements like these repeatedly in *Revival Lectures*, the *Autobiography*, and his *Systematic Theology*. Of course, the Bible teaches the opposite: ". . . Christ died for our sins . . ." (1 Corinthians 15:3).

Finney horribly misrepresented the atonement of Christ for our sins, and attacked the very foundation of the Gospel.

Is It a "Wonderful Theological Fiction"?

Closely connected with the blood atonement is the imputation of Christ's righteousness. Historically, Protestants and Baptists have believed that Christ's righteousness is given or "imputed" to men and women when they are converted. But Finney called the imputation of Christ's righteousness a "wonderful theological fiction."[23] He taught that Christ's righteousness is not given or imputed to sinners. He so strongly disagreed with imputation that he wrote,

"I could not but regard and treat this whole question of imputation as a theological fiction."[24] Again, Finney wrote: "His [Christ's] obedience could no more than justify Himself. It can never be imputed to us."[25]

He maintained the view that man saves himself by a series of decisions rather than through the imputed righteousness of Christ. Of course, the Bible teaches the opposite. Christ's righteousness is imputed to us when we are saved (Romans 4:5, 8).

Here Finney struck a blow at the very foundation of Protestant and Baptist beliefs. Justification by faith through the imputed righteousness of Christ was the *very* doctrine which separated the Reformers from the Catholics (whose beliefs were similar to those of Finney). The correct biblical view of justification, and imputation (which Finney rejected) was given by A. A. Hodge:

> The doctrine that justification is forensic [legal], and that it is based upon imputed righteousness was the watchword of the glorious Reformation—the one word of power which dissolved the venerable power of the Papacy.[26]

Luther agreed. He made the doctrine of the imputation of Christ's righteousness crystal clear:

> Righteousness, then, is such a faith and is called "God's righteousness," or "the righteousness that avails before God," because God gives it and counts it [imputes it] as righteousness for the sake of Christ, our Mediator.[27]

John Wesley was in full agreement with Hodge and Luther on this point:

> We are justified by faith, not by works. The meaning is, God justifies the believer for the sake of Christ's righteousness, and not for any righteousness of his own. So Calvin (Institutes 1, 2, c. 17) "Christ is our righteousness, that, upon our believing, we should

be accounted righteous [have Christ's righteousness imputed to us] by him." St. Paul affirms this over and over; therefore I affirm it too. Faith is imputed for righteousness to every believer.[28]

This quotation shows that John Wesley was in complete agreement with John Calvin on the imputation of Christ's righteousness and justification through faith in Jesus. Protestants and Baptists agreed on imputation before Finney.

John Bunyan, our Baptist theologian, author, and preacher, gave the same view as Hodge, Luther, Wesley, and Calvin:

I believe, we are sinful creatures in ourselves, that no good thing done by us, can procure of God the imputation of the righteousness of Christ. But the imputation thereof is an act of grace through the redemption that is in Christ Jesus. I believe that the offer of this [imputed] righteousness, as tendered in the gospel, is to be received by faith.[29]

Finney declared the imputation of Christ's righteousness "wonderful theological fiction."[30] He wrote: "I could not but regard and treat this whole question of imputation as a theological fiction."[31] Thus, Finney set himself against John Calvin, John Bunyan, John Wesley, A. A. Hodge, and the entire spectrum of Protestant and Baptist thought for over four hundred years. In fact, Finney had the arrogance to say, "Very little of the gospel has come out upon the world, for these hundreds of years, without being clogged and obscured by false theology."[32]

How Could All of Them Be Wrong?

How could Luther, Calvin, Bunyan, Wesley, and Hodge *have all been wrong* on justification by faith through the imputed righteousness of Christ? How could *all* the Protestants and Baptists have been wrong on this fundamental doctrine, and *only* Finney correct? *How can we agree that every Baptist and Protestant was wrong, waiting long centuries for Finney to come and correct them?*

The Bible itself proves that *Finney* was the one who was wrong (Romans 4:3–24):

> But to him that worketh not, but believeth on him that justifieth the ungodly, his faith is counted [imputed] for righteousness.
>
> —Romans 4:5

> But for us also, to whom it shall be imputed, if we believe on him that raised up Jesus our Lord from the dead.
>
> —Romans 4:24

It was not Luther, Calvin, Bunyan, Wesley or Hodge, who "clogged and obscured" biblical teaching concerning imputation and justification. It was Charles G. Finney who rejected the foundational Protestant and Baptist doctrine of justification by faith alone through the imputed righteousness of Christ. It was Charles G. Finney who called the views of the Reformation "theological fiction," and substituted for correct Bible doctrine his own false idea that sinners save themselves by "a change of choice." It was Finney who has led Protestants and Baptists back to Rome.

I have heard several thoughtful men say that Methodism is the root-source of decisionism. I believe this to be a false thesis. The Methodists, though off on other points, stuck to the basic teachings of the Reformation regarding the pivotal doctrines of justification and imputation. It was Finney who changed these doctrines. As Iain H. Murray points out, "Finney differed from the Methodists in at least one major respect. . . . They attempted no major reformulation of Christian doctrine."[33] No, it was Finney and his followers who paved the way toward the union with Rome that is unfolding in our time.

Finney Taught Catholics How to Get "Converts"

I have in my hand a book titled *Catholic Revivalism: The American Experience 1830–1900*, by Jay P. Dolan, associate professor of history at the University of Notre Dame.

This book proves that Charles G. Finney taught a leading Catholic priest how to bring people into the Catholic Church. On page fifteen of the introduction, Professor Dolan quotes a letter written by Finney, which the evangelist included in his memoirs:

Several of the lawyers that were present at this time converted in Rochester, gave up their profession and went into the ministry. Among these was one of Chancellor W [Walworth's] sons, at that time a young lawyer in Rochester, and who appeared at this time to be soundly converted. For some reason, with which I am not acquainted, he went to Europe and then to Rome, and finally became a Roman Catholic priest. He has been for many years laboring zealously to promote revivals of religion among them, holding protracted meetings; and, as he told me himself . . . trying to accomplish in the Roman Catholic Church what I was endeavoring to accomplish in the Protestant Church. . . . He said he was laboring among the Roman Catholics to promote revivals of religion.[34]

Professor Dolan writes: "The person to whom Finney referred was Clarence Walworth, lawyer, convert [of Finney's], Roman Catholic priest, and one of the foremost parish mission preachers in nineteenth-century Catholic America."[35]

The book goes on to show how Father Walworth brought Finney's techniques into Catholicism and used them to gain tens of thousands of Americans for the Catholic Church.

The connection between Walworth's apostolate as a parish minister and Finney's revival ministry very poignantly illustrates the main thesis of this study. The religion of revivalism was not exclusively a Protestant enterprise, but it also swept through Catholic America in the second half of the nineteenth century.[36]

Here are the methods Father Walworth learned from Finney:

Most Catholics are familiar with the parish mission. It was a time when a religious order preacher was invited to the parish to revive the religious vitality of the people. For a week or more the preacher would hammer home the saving truths of Christianity, urging people to repent and do penance for their sins. Groups of religious order preachers toured Catholic America conducting parish missions in an effort to revive the religion of the people.[37]

Catholic "Revivals"

Let us note several things:

1. The "parish mission" was the Catholic equivalent to a week's "revival" meetings, as conducted by Finney and his followers.

Professor Dolan writes:

> In this study "parish mission" and "Catholic revival meeting" are used interchangeably. The reasons for this are twofold. Nineteenth-century observers, Finney included, were quick to see the similiarity between the two phenomena and described the parish mission as a revival. In addition, the parish mission fostered a type of religion, evangelicalism, that has long been associated with the techniques of mass evangelism known as revivalism.[38]

2. These Catholic "revival meetings" were started by a man who was "converted" in Finney's 1842 "revival," held in Rochester, N.Y., a man named Father Clarence Walworth. This man continued to learn "revival" techniques from Finney for a number of years.
3. Father Walworth succeeded in making Finney's type of meetings an integral part of the Catholic Church, and tens of thousands were "converted" to Catholicism as a result.
4. The themes preached on in these Catholic "revivals" were similar to those of Finney: "repentance" as "penance."
5. The great Protestant and Baptist themes (which had been rejected by Finney) were never preached, such as

a. Total human depravity (Ephesians 4:18–19; Colossians 1:21).
b. Justification through a one-time trust in Jesus, i.e., conversion (Galatians 2:16).
c. The imputation of Christ's righteousness changing the sinner's standing before a Holy God, rather than merely changing his life on earth (Romans 5:1, 9).
d. Jesus as the mediator, the loving Son of God,who can be personally known as the only needed intercessor: This was not preached (1 Timothy 2:5–6; 1 Timothy 1:15; John 14:6).

In place of these great Protestant and Baptist themes, Finney and his Roman Catholic admirers preached:

1. The need for a human decision, rather than a conversion accomplished by God.
2. They also preached a system of good works, and repentance as penance, rather than that once-for-all washing of regeneration through the blood of Jesus.

There never was a real revival among Roman Catholics in the nineteenth or twentieth century, such as those recorded time after time in Protestant and Baptist history. Why? Simply because true revival does *not* come by "urging people to repent and do penance for their sins."[39]

Dr. Lloyd-Jones pointed out that there can be no real revival where total depravity, the centrality of Jesus, the blood of Jesus, justification by faith, and regeneration, rather than a decision, are not central.[40] Since all of those are exclusively Protestant doctrines, they cannot appear in Catholic preaching even today, and *did* not appear in the preaching of Father Walworth, Finney's convert and disciple.

What Father Walworth and his helpers *did* do, by directly copying Finney, was to build a machine that mass-produced people for the Catholic Church. "Catholic revivals reached the working class more successfully than did their Protestant counterparts."[41]

It should not surprise us, knowing this material, that Billy Graham was embraced by the Catholic Church in the late twentieth century. One hundred years of preparation, started by Finney's decisionist methods, and carried forth by Father Walworth and his helpers, lay behind Graham's inclusion of Catholics in his meeting. Catholics made up sixty percent or more of Graham's audiences. When he called them to come and "reconfirm their confirmation" or "repent," he was saying words they had heard for over a hundred years from Finney and his fellow decisionists like Father Clarence Walworth. Graham carefully avoided preaching on the great Protestant themes of total depravity, justification by a one-time trust in Christ, and the imputation of Christ's righteousness as strictly a change of standing before God, rather than merely a change of the individual. Thus, through Finney's influence, Graham preached subjects acceptable to Roman Catholics and avoided the great Protestant themes of the Reformation and the historic Baptists like the plague! In essence, Graham brought Finney's message to our generation: save yourself by a decision and dedicate yourself repeatedly. This is a far cry from the helpless state of the lost proclaimed by Baptists and Protestants in the glory days of real revival in the past.

What we hear today from Promise Keepers, Bill Bright, Chuck Colson, TBN, and almost all other prominent new evangelicals, is the message of decisionism, the message of Finney, perfectly acceptable to Roman Catholics, leading evangelicalism back to union with Rome.

Pollster George Barna shows how widely the Finney/Graham view of salvation by a decision is accepted among Roman Catholics today. An article in *Word* magazine is titled "A Rise in Born-Again Catholics." Here is what Barna discovered:

A growing number of U.S. Roman Catholics say they are born-again, according to pollster George Barna. In just two years, there has been a 41 percent increase. . . . The study involved a scientific sample of 1,007 adults nationwide.[42]

Finney and Graham's decisionist form of salvation is sweeping through the Roman Catholic Church and uniting the Catholics with decisionist Protestants. It is decisionism which is bringing about this union.

Salvation by a Decision

We have seen that Finney believed in repeated decisions, rather than a one-time conversion. He denied that Christ died for our sins. He denied the imputation of Christ's righteousness to the Christian. His teachings were so compatible with the Roman Catholic Church that they have fully embraced his methods and his message. Now, here is the next major doctrine Finney changed. *He preached salvation by human choice rather than conversion accomplished by God*. For the effect it has had on evangelicalism, this is *by far* the most serious error he taught. It has literally ruined the spiritual life of our nation, and brought us to a point where Billy Graham could say, "We are a society poised on the brink of self destruction."[43] Finney wrote:

Regeneration consists in the sinner changing his ultimate choice . . . in other words, a turning from the supreme choice of self-gratification to the supreme love of God . . . the work accomplished is a change of choice.[44]

Iain H. Murray said:

For Finney a *public action* had become an essential part of evangelism. He believed that all that was needed for conversion was a resolution signified by standing, kneeling, or coming forward, and because the Holy Spirit always acts when a sinner acts, the public resolution could be treated as "identical with the miraculous inward change of sudden conversion."[45]

That is not Protestant or Baptist teaching. It is similar to what the heretic Pelagius taught in the fifth century, the heresy of Pelagianism.

H. C. Thiessen gives a far more scriptural definition of regeneration: "We may define regeneration as the communication of divine life to the soul."[46] That is orthodox, scriptural teaching regarding the new birth. Before Finney, all Protestants and Baptists believed this. They believed that conversion was something *God* did to you. Finney changed this to something that *you* do out of obedience to God.

The old Gospel taught that man was lost and needed to be saved, because he couldn't save himself. Finney's "new" gospel taught that man could save *himself* because he wasn't really lost. Man could save himself by a "choice" or decision. He did not need Jesus to die for his sins. And because man was strong enough to save himself, he could also lose his salvation, repeatedly, even after he got to Heaven!

Thus, Finney taught that man did not need Jesus at all, in any real, ontological sense. Man could obey God and save himself. This is not Christ-centered theology. It is Pelagianism. C. H. Spurgeon said, "We do not often agree with Mr. Finney's theology."[47] Spurgeon's assistant, V. J. Charlesworth, said, "It would need a lengthy paper to combat the Pelagian heresy which is so conspicuous in these quotations" [from Finney].[48]

Some have called Finney a semi-Pelagianist, but this is an error. A careful study of his work reveals he is a thorough going Pelagian heretic, as Rev. Charlesworth indicated. This heresy has permeated much of evangelicalism in our day. Although most evangelicals would reject several of Finney's ideas, yet many of these same people embrace his false theory of decisionism. They should see *where* these doctrines of decisionism came from, and where they lead— into the arms of the Catholic Church.

It was Finney who rejected the great doctrines of the Reformation and opened the door for evangelicals to take his decisionist road back to Rome. By chopping out the imputation of Christ's righteousness, the total depravity of man, and justification solely by faith in Jesus, Finney cut away the foundational teachings of all basic Protestant and Baptist thought. That is why so many evangelical preachers themselves are lost. They have tried one form or another of the Catholic/Finney plan of salvation, the Pelagian plan of decisionism.

Finney wrote: "Men are to be converted, not by a change wrought in their nature or constitution by creative power, but by the truth made effectual by the Holy Ghost."[49] He asked: "What is regeneration? What is it but the beginning of obedience to God?"[50] "When an individual actually chooses to obey God, he is a Christian."[51] *A Muslim could say that. A Jehovah's Witness could say that. And many modern evangelicals do say that!* Finney says: "What is regeneration? What is it but a new beginning of obedience to God?" Thiessen said: "We may define regeneration as the communication of divine life to the soul." *These are two opposite ideas. Things that are different are not the same!*

Several elements are missing in Finney's decisionist view of conversion:

1. No mention of the mediatorial work of Jesus Christ (1 Timothy 2:5; John 14:6).
2. No mention of sin (1 Timothy 1:15).
3. No mention of the blood of Jesus washing sins away (1 John 1:7).
4. No mention of the Gospel of Christ (1 Corinthians 15:1–4).

Perhaps a person could trust Jesus and not mention those four points in his testimony. However, it seems to me that Finney should have put much more emphasis on what Jesus does *for* us. The great evangelist Asahel Nettleton, the man who opposed Finney, said this: "We see why it is that sinners say so little about the Saviour. They do not feel that they are lost. They that are whole, need not a physician, but they that are sick."[52]

Finney himself was quite aware that he was changing what Baptists and Protestants had always believed about conversion. Iain H. Murray writes:

> Finney himself was deeply conscious of the radical contrast between his own preaching and the orthodoxy of his day. By 1835 he was ready to tell his hearers that he was presenting what was virtually a new theology of conversion: "The truth is that very little of the Gospel has come out upon the world, for these hundreds of years, without being clogged and obscured by false theology." And he made clear the very point that Nettleton had been one of the first to suspect, that the new measures* were to be defended on the basis of a new theology.[53]

Murray is correct. Finney changed evangelicalism. The old belief of conversion, that brought with it three great periods of revival, was changed by Finney into the decisionism that is common throughout the Western world today.

Satan Attacks Conversion Through Finney and His Followers
I believe that Satan used Charles G. Finney to destroy the old religion of revival and bring in the new religion of decisionism— the road back to Rome. I am not alone in my belief that Satan used Finney. Bennet Tyler wrote a biography of Asahel Nettleton, published in 1854. In it, Tyler wrote:

> Revivals have never been permitted by Satan to continue long without some direct effort on his part to counterwork them. And so it was to be now. The form of this attack was crafty; it was made by assuming the form of an angel of light . . . occasioned principally by the Rev. Charles G. Finney.[54]

Satan used Finney as "an angel of light" to bring decisionism to our churches and lead us to ruin and to Catholicism.

---

* Coming forward to make a public profession, etc.

With Finney's new religion of decisionism, everyone who has made *any sort* of decision is now accepted as a Christian and as a member of the "universal church" in the eyes of new evangelicals. No wonder Charles Colson, Bill Bright, Pat Robertson, and J. I. Packer have issued a document called "Evangelicals and Catholics Together," which declares that all active Catholics are our "brothers and sisters in Christ."[55] They have been brought to this position by the decisionism of Charles G. Finney. Mr. Colson and Dr. Packer say they hold Reformation doctrine, but *in practice* they are decisionists. Thus, decisionism has become the road back to Catholicism in our time.

But the old way of conversion is the only way to Heaven. Jesus said:

. . . Except a man be born again, he cannot see the kingdom of God. . . .

—John 3:3

Marvel not that I said unto thee, Ye must be born again.

—John 3:7

. . . Verily I say unto you, Except ye be converted, and become as little children, ye shall not enter into the kingdom of heaven. . . .

—Matthew 18:3

A friend of mine read the manuscript of this book and then said that he always wondered how the churches moved so quickly from revival to apostasy, "from Philadelphia to Laodicea," as he put it. After reading this book, *he now believes Satan used Charles Finney to bring in the end-time apostasy*. That is an interesting position, worthy of far more attention than is possible to devote to it now. Jesus said, ". . . Many false prophets shall rise, and shall deceive many . . ." (Matthew 24:11).

Needed: A Converted Church Membership

In 1903 the American Baptist Publication Society published a book titled *The Great Awakening of 1740*, by Rev. F. L. Chapell. This book was issued by the old Northern Baptist Convention (later called the American Baptist Convention), and Rev. Chapell was a mainstream Northern Baptist in 1903. Chapell's book reveals that the situation before the First Great Awakening was similar to our day in many ways:

> The voice of the few and scattered Baptists was raised from time to time in favor of a converted church-membership, but with little general effect since they had no legal or influential standing. . . . The churches themselves were in a very low state of spiritual life and power, since a large portion of their members knew nothing of that heart experience which constitutes the essence of true religion. . . . Thus it came to pass that there were not only unconverted and unspiritual men in the ministry, but there were found leading and prominent divines to argue that such a state of things was perfectly proper, that it was not necessary to have an experimental knowledge of religion (i.e. conversion) in order to preach it. . . . People heard scarcely anything in many cases from the pulpit that was at all searching, for a dead ministry must, of course, preach dead sermons. But if the truth did sometimes fall upon the people, it had but little effect, when they remembered that they . . . had fulfilled the requirements of the church. They considered that they were Christians already, in some sense. . . . The general result was, of course, that the need of conversion was practically denied. Such was the state of the best, or at least the most influential portion of Protestantism in the earlier years of the eighteenth century. . . . You will see that to human view Christianity was clean gone forever. The floods of ungodly men were sweeping on, and a corrupt and enervated church [was the result]. Numbers of them held at this time, that it was quite difficult, in fact impossible, to discover from the affections whether regeneration had taken place or not. . . . A conscious experience of the regenerating work of the Holy Spirit was not insisted upon. . . . The cornerstone of the Baptist faith is a professedly converted church-membership. Before the

Great Awakening, none except Baptists acknowledged this principle. . . . The dark days that preceded the Great Awakening will
come again unless somebody stands firmly and clearly and decidedly by the doctrine of a converted church-membership.[56]

The words that Rev. Chapell wrote in 1903 have come true. We
need to stand for the old Baptist doctrine of conversion: "The dark
days that preceded the Great Awakening will come again unless
somebody stands firmly and clearly and decidedly by the doctrine
of a converted church-membership."[57]

These terrible days are characterized by literally millions of lost
church members. Did you know that one-half of the nation's fifteen million Southern Baptists give less than one dollar a year in
church? Did you know that one-half of these fifteen million Baptists did not attend church even one time last year?[58] Thomas Ascol,
an SBC pastor and author, blames the "modern evangelistic technique, geared toward getting a sinner to agree with some facts and
recite a prayer."[59] He claims that decisionist methods have produced the Southern Baptist Convention, with a full fifteen million
members, many of whom never attend church, and many of whom
give less than a dollar apiece each year.

The situation in the Southern Baptist Convention reveals problems which exist in all evangelical churches. The SBC is the mir-
ror-image of evangelicalism in general. When you see a major error in the SBC, you can be quite sure it also exists in evangelicalism
at large.

Jesus gave this prophetic warning: "And many false prophets
shall rise, and shall deceive many. And because iniquity shall
abound, the love of many shall wax [grow] cold" (Matthew 24:11–
12).

Verse eleven tells us that "false prophets shall rise, and shall
deceive many." Verse twelve shows us that "iniquity" (Greek:
anomian = lawlessness) will "abound" and that this will cause the
love (Greek: *agapé* = Christian love) of Christians to grow cold.
The "iniquity" of the last days is a direct product of the deceptions

of the false prophets in the previous verse. *The coldness of real Christians is a result of the chaotic lawlessness of the unconverted members of the churches to which they belong.*

Churches fill up with those who practice fornication, covetousness, railing, drunkenness, extortion, etc. (1 Corinthians 5:11). Most churches today refuse to obey 1 Corinthians 5:13 and "put away from among yourselves that wicked person." Since this is not done very often in our day, the local churches have become literal hot-beds of iniquity, and bring great discouragement to the few members, the small remnant, who are truly converted. "And because iniquity shall abound, the love of many shall wax cold."

Southern Baptist Chaos

A study conducted by the Home Mission Board of the Southern Baptist Convention reveals that more than sixty percent of adults baptized in Southern Baptist churches have been baptized before.[60] Out of one hundred fifty thousand adult baptisms, only sixty thousand represented baptisms for first-time professions. This means only four out of ten were first-time professions. The other six out of ten were baptized before and were "rededicating their lives." Their baptisms were based on rededictions. The article said, *"The survey indicates the need for more counselling of those seeking baptism."*[61] The report goes on to ask these pointed questions:

> Are pastors assuming the responsibility for clarifying the response of the people to the invitation call? Is the pressure to baptize so great that pastors are encouraging people to be baptized rather than counselling them on [conversion]? The study should challenge any assumption that most adults baptized are recent converts. Thus, baptisms are not an accurate count of conversions.[62]

Thomas Wright, of the SBC Home Mission Board, said that the survey indicates that *"we are not carefully counselling those who indicate an interest in becoming Christians."*[63]

Forty percent came forward for salvation and were baptized. Forty percent came forward for rededication and were baptized. Fourteen percent came forward to transfer membership and were baptized. Six percent came forward for some other reason and were baptized. "Of those who were rebaptized, 35.8 percent were receiving their second immersion in a Southern Baptist church."[64] One famous Baptist church has baptized its Sunday school students an average of *five* times each! In other words—total confusion. This is one of the results of decades of decisionism.

It should be remembered that these facts and figures from the SBC are the same as virtually all evangelical churches in general. They are mostly a replication of what is happening in the other evangelical groups.

C. H. Spurgeon wrote:

> Conversions are thought to be easy things by a certain enthusiastic school* and truly they ought to be, for they are soon over. We have known men converted just long enough to become apostates. . . . Conversion is something more than this. It is a divine work.[65]

Pulpit Helps gives a succinct account of the changes brought about by Finney and his followers:

> Finney was to bring in new methods and a new attitude t o w a r d revival. Jonathan Edwards had viewed the 1735 revival at Northampton as "a very extraordinary dispensation Providence," a "surprising work of God." Charles G. Finney, however, believed that "a revival is not a miracle. It is a purely [scientific] result of the right use of the constituted means." In the series of revivals Finney held from 1824–1837, Finney instituted a number of new measures which later evangelists would continue. These included advertising and advanced preparation for the revival meeting. Finney pressed for decisions. He was the first to have an "invitation," call-

---

* i.e., decisionists.

ing people to the front to make a public witness to their conversion.[66]

The two main changes Finney brought to the evangelical churches were these:

1. Revivals are not miracles (and neither are individual conversions).
2. Response to the "invitation" is conversion (rather than the inward work of God).

Both points reveal the man-centered position of Finney, and both have come into mainstream evangelicalism so strongly that many people now feel that these false ideas have always been held by Christians. This is, of course, the result of ignoring history.

Revivals *Are* Miracles

Finney's idea that "revival is not a miracle" has brought great harm to evangelicalism, first, because it is not true, and second, because it is not scriptural. I do not mean to say that the two are separate. I am saying it is not true that revivals are only the natural result of using the right methods. Since it is not true, it does not work. Since it does not work, most churches have all but given up any emphasis on revival in our day. *Finney's methods just don't work. They do not produce real converts.* Second, the idea that revivals are only the natural result of using the right methods is unscriptural. Jesus said: "The wind bloweth where it listeth, and thou hearest the sound thereof, but canst not tell whence it cometh, and whither it goeth . . ." (John 3:8).

There is a supernatural quality in genuine revivals. In Acts 2:37 the unconverted were "pricked in the heart" as the result of a sermon. But in Acts 7:54 another group were "cut to the heart" and stoned the preacher to death. The second preacher was ". . . full of the Holy Ghost . . ." (Acts 7:55), but his preaching fell·on deaf ears even though he used the same method (or "measure," as Finney would say) as the first preacher.

So, Finney's teaching that there is nothing whatever miraculous in revival is not true to the Bible. This doctrine brings great harm by leading people to think that individual conversions are not miraculous either. These "conversions" are simply the "result of the right use" of Finney's methods. But Jesus said, ". . . so is every one that is born of the Spirit" (John 3:8). A person is born again by the miraculous intervention of the Holy Spirit, not by the human effort of saying a prayer or making a decision of any kind, including mere mental belief in the plan of salvation, or a "Lordship" commitment.

The Invitation

Pulpit Helps correctly says: "Finney instituted a number of new measures which later evangelists would continue. He was the first to have an 'invitation,' calling people to the front."[66] There are several observations to be made concerning this statement:

1. The greatest evangelists of all time never gave a Finney-like public invitation. Jesus never gave one. Peter never gave one. Paul never gave one. Luther never gave one. Whitefield never gave one. Wesley never gave one. Bunyan never gave one. Spurgeon never gave one. In fact, Christianity went on for over eighteen hundred years before Finney promoted the "public invitation to accept Christ" for the first time in history!
2. The greatest revivals of history occurred with no public invitations.
3. There has never been any major revival where the public invitation was used, only perhaps local ones, but nothing ever on the scale of the Great Awakenings, after Finney introduced this technique.

Now, having said that, it is my own personal belief that the public invitation itself is not what needs to be given up. I have personally seen people converted (1) without any public invitation, and (2) with various types of public invitations (hands raised, coming forward, etc.). I have therefore concluded that the invitation *itself* is not the basis of the problem today. *The mistakes in our time occur in what is said during the invitation, and what is done afterwards.* It is often assumed that the response to the invitation is *itself* conversion, and so all who respond are baptized instantly and received into the churches. Others take just a moment or two, during the confusion of the altar call, to go over the points of salvation. Little beyond these two methods is seen today.

If some pastors are persuaded to consider dealing more closely and personally with those who respond to the invitation, the effort of writing this book will not have been in vain. We do not expect our methods to be followed exactly. Each pastor will have to decide for himself what to modify. We do not think our ideas are perfect. We are still learning. Suggestions for improvement will be received heartily.

Here is the method we have adopted in our church. First, I make the Gospel as clear as possible in the sermon. At least the conclusion, if not the entire message, is devoted to this, though my sermons are nearly all completely evangelistic.

1. I explain what sin is and make it as clear as possible that those who are unconverted are lost.
2. I give the invitation. This is done with little or no emotion. I do not use "heart tugging stories." I find that excessive emotion here only confuses the lost. I want the emphasis to be on their need for Jesus to forgive their sins.
3. I give the invitation in one of two ways:
   a. I ask them to come to the front if they want to talk to me in my office about having their sins forgiven by Jesus. I am careful to use *these* words. I do *not* say, "Come to Jesus," or anything like that. This tends toward decisionism. I just tell them to come *so we can talk in my office* about Jesus forgiving their sins. Then those who come regularly sing a stanza or two of an invitation hymn. After a stanza or two, trained workers speak to the unconverted and gently ask

them to go forward. Usually several have already responded. We do a great deal of work every week before each Sunday service, so there are always people who respond. Usually about half of those who come do so before the workers speak to them.

b. At other times I do not give the above invitation at all. Instead, I ask the people to pray at the end of the sermon. While they pray, the workers lead the unconverted out of the auditorium to my office. It brings freshness to our services to alternate these methods from time to time, as they best fit the sermon.

4. The unconverted are taken to an office next to mine and are given a sheet of paper to read. This sheet is reproduced on page 128.

5. Then Dr. Cagan, my associate, and I speak to them one by one in my office. One other trained worker who speaks Spanish is present as well. He has done this for many years. *We do not use anyone else for this delicate and important work*, except our deacon, Benjamin Kincaid Griffith, who presides over this room, and deals with some special cases I assign to him. Dr. Cagan, one of my sons, and a woman in our church also help us. I am in charge of the entire procedure, which usually lasts about forty minutes directly after each service. Our people know where I am, and they know they can come into my office and see me at this time if absolutely necessary. I do not shake hands with people at the door after the services. The people know that I am dealing with the lost at this time.

I *strongly* disagree with the "shotgun" approach to the invitation, where people are urged to come forward "to get saved, to join the church, to rededicate their life, to join the choir, to transfer a letter, etc." The appeal should be to the lost *alone*. Then, when this appeal has been explained thoroughly and given, the other appeals may be added. If no one comes for salvation, don't be disconcerted. Counsel the others in your inquiry room or office. But the next week do your "homework" and prepare several other people to walk the aisle the next Sunday so you can talk to them in a quiet place.

Many preachers take Saturday off or use it to prepare sermons. To me this is a mistake. I take Monday off with my family and use Tuesday to prepare the sermons for the following Sunday. I prepare the outlines on Tuesday. This gives me four days to think about them and add illustrations before Sunday. It also gives time for my sermon notes to be translated into Spanish and Chinese.

Friday, and especially Saturday, should be used for phoning and visiting the lost, to get them to church on Sunday. Do as much of this work yourself on Friday and Saturday as possible. Arrange to pick up some of these new prospects yourself, in your own car. Later you can delegate some of this work. My wife picks up new people in her car every Sunday morning and evening, as do many other members of our church. There will always be lost people in every service if this is done vigorously.

Pastors themselves need to deal directly with the lost after they preach, in a quiet, undisturbed situation, perhaps in their own office. At some point, I deal with every inquirer before they are baptized. I do this several times with each person, to make certain they are converted. *That is really the most important point we are attempting to make in this book.* It is the type of ministry our Lord did with the woman at the well in John 4:6–29; with the rich young ruler in Mark 10:17–31; with Zacchaeus in Luke 19:1–10; with the man born blind in John 9:1–38; with Simon the Pharisee in Luke 7:36–50; and with many others. Even if nothing else we have written is done, I believe that *personal work by the pastor will greatly help in reversing the terrible effects of decisionism.*

Ephesians 4:11–12 tells us that Jesus gave pastors and leaders in the local church ". . . for the perfecting of the saints, for the work of the ministry, for the edifying of the body of Christ." Surely this "perfecting" and "edifying of the body" begins with leading people into a genuine conversion. Ephesians 4:11–12 says, in part, "He gave some . . . pastors . . . for the edifying of the body of Christ." Expositor W. E. Vine tells us that the word translated edifying is *oikodome*, and that it "denotes the act of building a home."[67] This same Greek word is used at the end of Ephesians 4:16: ". . . maketh increase of the body unto the edifying [*oikodome*] of itself in love." Both verses refer to evangelism as well as discipleship. So, pastors are given by Jesus (4:11) to build the local church body, by leading souls into conversion, since edifying "denotes the act of building a home" and that home is ". . . the body of Christ, . . ." the local church (Ephesians 4:12, 16).

If these were the only verses that taught pastors to build up their churches through preaching and personal evangelism it would be enough. But other passages, such as Romans 10:14 tell us, ". . . How shall they hear without a preacher? . . ." The Holy Spirit records the eunuch's question to Philip, "How can I, except some man should guide me?" (Acts 8:31).

When these and other verses are coupled with the example of Jesus, as in the passages already cited, we have a very strong case from the Bible for pastors taking time alone with the lost, to make absolutely certain they are converted.

We must love the lost enough to get to know them personally. We must love them enough to weep and pray with them—and *listen* to what they believe.

6. As I sit down with each person, I introduce myself and then I ask them, "What do you want Jesus to do for you today?" If the answer they give has anything to do with forgiveness of sins, I proceed with the Gospel.

The methods used by the prince of preachers, C. H. Spurgeon, are well worth reviewing in this day of decisionism. Here is the way he added members to his vast congregation:

Candidates for church membership have an interview with one of the Elders,* some of whom attend the Tabernacle for that purpose every Wednesday evening.** A record is made by the Elder of the result of that interview in what is called the Inquirer's Book. If satisfied with the candidate, he gives a card, which qualifies for direct intercourse with Mr. Spurgeon, who devotes a fixed portion of that time to his office. If Mr. Spurgeon thinks favorably of that individual, the name is announced at a church meeting, and visitors are appointed to make the most careful inquiries into the whole circumstances connected with the application [for membership]. If this investigation is satisfactory, the candidate appears at a church meeting where he is examined by the Pastor, after which he retires, and the visitor gives his report upon the case. It is then proposed to the Church for its adoption, and if approved, the Pastor gives the right hand of fellowship. As soon after this as convenient, the candidate is baptized, and on the next first Sabbath in the month ensuing, unites in the Communion Service, having first been recognized before the whole Church by again receiving from the Pastor the right hand of fellowship.[68]

Without going into great detail in reviewing this narrative, I think you will see instantly that it stands in stark contrast to the decisionist way of receiving people for baptism today. I recommend that you read the paragraph on Spurgeon's methods again—slowly. ***Think carefully about the way people are received and baptized into your church. Then ask yourself if more effort in spending time with those seeking salvation might not produce more real converts in your church.***

Spurgeon's methods were typical of the old-time methods of Baptists. Eric W. Hayden gives insight on the great preacher's meth-

---

* Spurgeon's Tabernacle was (and is) a Baptist Church. These "elders" did not govern the church, but were appointed for one year. Their duties were confined to soul winning and visitation work. The church did ***not*** have elder rule.

** The prayer meeting was held on Monday evenings at the Tabernacle. Wednesday night was largely devoted to dealing with anxious sinners.

ods in an article on Spurgeon's weekly schedule. Here is a synopsis:

> After the Sunday services he often remained at the Tabernacle for another hour while he interviewed enquirer.s* . . . From seven until half-past eight at night [on Mondays] he would be interviewing enquirers prior to the Monday evening prayer meeting at the Tabernacle. Talking with enquirers he called "glorious work."[69]

I have read elsewhere that he often spent time on other nights of the week "interviewing enquirers." Remember, Spurgeon baptized no one into his huge church without *personally* being certain that the man or woman was converted.

I am convinced that we need to return to this sort of personal work. This was done by Jesus Himself. In John 3:1–21 Jesus gave a personal interview to Nicodemus. In John 4:7–30 Jesus gave a personal interview to the woman at the well. We listed earlier several other instances of our Lord doing such personal work. These were exactly the kind of interviews the old Baptist and Protestant pastors gave to inquirers before the change under Finney's decisionism ruined evangelicalism.

There are many other instances of such personal interviews with Jesus and the apostles recorded in the Bible. *How can pastors today do the work of Jesus and the apostles without following the example of Jesus and the apostles on this matter? Pastors must spend much time individually with each lost person.*

Footnotes

1. Iain H. Murray, *Revival and Revivalism,* p. 297.
2. Ibid.
3. Ibid., p. 298.
4. Ibid., p. 348.
5. Vernon J. Charlesworth, *The Sword and the Trowel,* May 1876, page 218.
6. Charles G. Finney, *Finney's Systematic Theology* (Minneapolis: Bethany House Publishers, 1994 reprint of 1878 edition), p. 543.

---

* Inquirers was spelled "enquirers" in nineteenth century England.

7. Ibid.
8. Ibid.
9. *Evangelicals and Catholics Together: The Mission in the Third Millennium,* reprinted by Dr. D. A. Waite, The Bible for Today, Collingswood, New Jersey, no date.
10. *What in the World!,* published by Bob Jones University, Greenville, SC, volume 19, number 1.
11. H. E. Jacobs, quoted in G. H. Gerberding, *The Way of Salvation in the Lutheran Church* (Philadelphia: Lutheran Publication Society, 1887), p. 215.
12. *Sword of the Lord,* September 19, 1997, p. 24.
13. *Word* magazine, October 18, 1997, p. 14.
14. Ibid.
15. *Finney's Systematic Theology,* p. 508.
16. Charles G. Finney, *An Autobiography* (Old Tappan, NJ: Fleming H. Revell, 1876), p. 50–51.
17. Ibid.
18. *Finney's Systematic Theology,* p. 373.
19. *Finney's Systematic Theology,* p. 375.
20. *Finney's Systematic Theology,* pp. 361–62.
21. Michael S. Horton, "The Legacy of Charles Finney," from *Modern Reformation* magazine, computer net posting, April 1, 1996.
22. Charles G. Finney, *An Autobiography,* p. 50–51.
23. Ibid., p. 57.
24. Ibid., p. 58.
25. *Finney's Systematic Theology,* p. 363.
26. A. A. Hodge, *The Atonement* (Memphis, TN: Footstool Publications, 1987), pp. 217–18.
27. Martin Luther, "Preface to the Epistle to the Romans," in *Works of Martin Luther* (Grand Rapids, MI: Baker Book House, 1982), p. 452.
28. John Wesley, *The Works of John Wesley* (Grand Rapids, MI: Baker Book House, third edition, 1979), volume V, pp. 240–41.
29. John Bunyan, *The Works of John Bunyan* (Edinburgh: Banner of Truth Trust, 1991), p. 597.
30. Charles G. Finney, *An Autobiography,* p. 57.
31. Ibid., p. 58.
32. Charles G. Finney, quoted in Iain H. Murray, *Revival and Revivalism: The Making and Marring of American Evangelicalism 1750–1858* (Edinburgh: Banner of Truth Trust, 1994), p. 246.
33. Murray, ibid., p. 259.
34. Charles G. Finney, *Memoirs,* quoted by Jay P. Dolan, *Catholic Revivalism: The American Experience 1830-1900* (Notre Dame, IN: University of Notre Dame Press, 1978), xv.
35. Jay P. Dolan, *Catholic Revivalism: The American Experience 1830–1900,* xv.
36. Ibid., xv–xvi.
37. Ibid., xvi.
38. Ibid.

39. Ibid.
40. D. Martyn Lloyd-Jones, *Revival* (Wheaton, IL: Crossway Books, 1987), pp. 35, 56–57.
41. Dolan, jacket comment, University of Notre Dame Press.
42. *Word* magazine, September 20, 1997, p. 19.
43. *Los Angeles Times,* May 3, 1996, p. A-10.
44. *Finney's Systematic Theology,* pp. 274–75.
45. Murray, p. 250.
46. Henry C. Thiessen, *Lectures in Systematic Theology* (Grand Rapids, MI: Wm. B. Eerdmans Publishing Co., 1949), p. 367.
47. C. H. Spurgeon, *The Sword and the Trowel,* July 1884, p. 439.
48. V. J. Charlesworth, *The Sword and the Trowel,* May 1876, p. 218.
49. Charles G. Finney, *Lectures on Revivals of Religion* (New York and London, 1910), p. 377.
50. Ibid., p. 383.
51. Ibid., p. 424.
52. Asahel Nettleton, *Sermons from the Second Great Awakening* (Ames, IA: International Outreach, 1995 reprint), p. 448.
53. Murray, p. 246.
54. Bennet Tyler and Andrew A. Bonar, *The Life and Labours of Asahel Nettleton* (Edinburgh: The Banner of Truth Trust, 1975 reprint of the 1854 edition), p. 339.
55. Dave Hunt, *The Berean Call,* April 1997, p. 3.
56. F. L. Chapell, *The Great Awakening of 1740* (Philadelphia: American Baptist Publication Society, 1903), pp. 18–21, 69, 132–133.
57. Ibid., p. 133.
58. *National and International Religion Report,* February 20, 1995, p. 5.
59. Ibid.
60. "Study: 60 Percent of Adult SBC Baptisms are Rebaptisms," compiled by Baptist Press, in *The California Southern Baptist,* May 4, 1995, p. 8.
61. Ibid.
62. Ibid.
63. Ibid.
64. Ibid.
65. C. H. Spurgeon in *Sword and the Trowel* (Pasadena, TX: Pilgrim Publications, 1983), volume V, 1877, p. 20.
66. *Pulpit Helps,* March 1996, p. 20.
67. W. E. Vine, *An Expository Dictionary of New Testament Words,* Volume II (Old Tappan, NJ: Fleming H. Revell Co., 1966), pp. 17–18.
68. Metropolitan Tabernacle Statistics," in *Sword and the Trowel, Volume One: Years 1865, 1866, 1867* (Pasadena, TX: Pilgrim Publications, 1975), year 1865, p. 31.
69. Eric W. Hayden, "Spurgeon's Working Week," from the jacket of volumes 62 and 63, *Metropolitan Tabernacle Pulpit,* 1916–1917 (Pasadena, TX: Pilgrim Publications, 1980).

Chapter Six

The Source of the Cesspool

But there were false prophets also among the people, even as there shall be false teachers among you, who privily shall bring in damnable heresies, even denying the Lord that bought them. . . .

—2 Peter 2:1

In Finney's theology, God is not sovereign; man is not a sinner by nature; the atonement is not a true payment for sin; justification by imputation is insulting to reason and morality; the new birth is simply the result of successful techniques, and revival is a natural result of clever campaigns.

—Dr. Michael S. Horton

He is not only an enemy of evangelical Protestantism, but of historic Christianity.

—Dr. Michael S. Horton

Michael S. Horton is the president of Christians United for Reformation. He is a graduate of Biola University and has a Ph.D. from Oxford University. He is the author of eight books, including *The Agony of Deceit*, an exposé of the charismatic "faith" teachers, Kenneth Copeland, Kenneth Hagin, and Frederick K. Price. Here is a synopsis of an article on Charles G. Finney by Dr. Horton:

Jerry Falwell calls him "one of my heroes and a hero to many evangelicals, including Billy Graham." I recall wandering through the Billy Graham Center some years ago, observing the place of honor given to Finney in the evangelical tradition, reinforced by the first class I had in theology at a Christian college, where Finney's work was required reading. The New York revivalist was the oft-quoted and celebrated champion of the Christian singer Keith Green and the Youth With a Mission organization. Finney is particularly esteemed among the leaders of the Christian Right and the Christian Left, by both Jerry Falwell and Jim Wallis (*Sojourners* magazine), and his imprint can be seen in movements that appear to be diverse, but in reality are merely heirs to Finney's legacy. From the Vineyard movement and the church growth movement to the political and social crusades, televangelism, and the Promise Keepers movement, as a former Wheaton College president rather glowingly cheered, "Finney lives on!"

Evangelists pitched their American gospel in terms of its practical usefulness to the individual and the nation. That is why Finney is so popular. He is the tallest marker in the shift from Reformation orthodoxy, evident in the Great Awakening [under Edwards and Whitefield] to . . . Pelagian revivalism. To demonstrate the debt of modern evangelicalism to Finney, we must first notice his theological departures. *From these departures, Finney became the father of the antecedents to some of today's greatest challenges within the evangelical churches themselves: namely, the church growth movement, pentecostalism and political revivalism.*

Who was Finney? Reacting against the [Protestant theology] of the Great Awakening, [Finney] turned from God to humans, from the preaching of objective content (namely, Christ and Him crucified) to the emphasis on getting a person to "make a decision."

Finney began conducting revivals in upstate New York. *One of his most popular sermons was, "Sinners Bound to Change Their Own Hearts."*

His "New Measures" included the "anxious bench" (precursor to today's altar call), emotional tactics that led to fainting and weeping, and other "excitements," as Finney and his followers called them.

What's So Wrong With Finney's Theology?

First, one need go no further than the table of contents of his *Systematic Theology* to learn that Finney's entire theology revolved around human morality. Finney did not really write a *Systematic Theology,* but a collection of essays on ethics. But that is not to say that Finney's *Systematic Theology* does not contain some significant theological statements.

When posed with the question, "Does a Christian cease to be a Christian, whenever he commits a sin?" Finney answers: "Whenever he sins, he must, for the time being, cease to be holy. This is self-evident. Whenever he sins, he must be condemned; he must incur the penalty of the law of God" (p. 46).

Finney declares of the Reformation's formula "simultaneously justified and sinful." "This error has slain more souls, I fear, than all the universalism that ever cursed the world." For, *"Whenever a Christian sins he comes under condemnation, and must repent and do his first works, or be lost"* (p. 60).

We will return to Finney's doctrine of justification, but it must be noted that it rests upon a denial of the doctrine of original sin. This biblical teaching insists that we are all born into this world inheriting Adam's guilt and corruption. But Finney followed Pelagius, the fifth-century heretic, in denying this doctrine.

Instead, Finney believed that human beings were capable of choosing whether they would be corrupt by nature or redeemed, referring to original sin as an "anti-scriptural and nonsensical dogma" (p. 179). In clear terms, Finney denied the notion that human beings possess a sinful nature (ibid.). Therefore, if Adam leads us into sin, not by our inheriting his guilt and corruption, but by following his poor example, this leads logically to the view of Christ, the Second Adam, as saving by example. This is precisely where Finney takes it, in his explanation of the atonement.*

---

* It is clear from the above material by Dr. Horton that Finney was a complete Pelagian. He did not believe that human nature was ruined by the fall. He believed that man's will is free at all times. This is a denial of the Protestant and Baptist doctrine of original sin, and its fruit (i.e. total depravity).

The first thing we must note about the atonement, Finney says, is that *Christ could not have died for anyone else's sins than his own.* * Finney did believe that Christ died for something—not for someone, but for something. In other words, he died for a purpose, but not for people. *The purpose of that death was to reassert God's moral government and to lead us to eternal life by example,* as Adam's example excited us to sin.

Having nothing to do with original sin, a substitutionary atonement, and the supernatural character of the new birth, Finney proceeds to attack "the article by which the church stands or falls"—justification by grace alone through faith alone.

The Protestant Reformers insisted, on the basis of clear biblical texts, that justification (in the Greek, "to declare righteous," rather than "to make righteous") was a forensic (i.e., "legal") verdict. In other words, whereas Rome maintained that justification was a process of making a bad person better, the Reformers argued that it was a declaration or pronouncement that had someone else's righteousness (i.e., Christ's) as its basis. Therefore, it was a perfect, once-for-all verdict of right-standing at the beginning of the Christian life, not in the middle or at the end.

To this, Finney replied, "The doctrine of an imputed righteousness, or that Christ's obedience to the law was accounted as our obedience, is founded on a most false and nonsensical assumption." After all, Christ's righteousness "could do no more than justify himself. It can never be imputed to us . . ." (pp. 320–22).

---

* Dr. Horton paraphrases Finney from pp. 219, 362 and 363 of *Finney's Systematic Theology* (Minneapolis, MN: Bethany House Publishers, 1994). For instance, Finney said, "His [Christ's] obedience could no more than justify Himself" (*Systematic Theology,* p. 363). Finney said, "Justification is not founded in Christ's literally suffering the exact penalty of the law and purchasing eternal salvation" (*Systematic Theology,* p. 373). "You cannot find in your heart to demand 'exact justice' at the hand of God, on the ground that Christ has literally paid your debt. To represent the work and death of Christ as the ground of justification in this sense is a snare and a stumbling-block" (*Systematic Theology,* p. 375).

The view that faith is the sole condition of justification is "the antinomian view," Finney asserts. "We shall see that perseverance in obedience to the end of life is also a condition of justification" (pp. 326–27). Each act of sin requires "a fresh justification" (p. 331).

His "New Measures," like today's church growth movement, made human choices and emotions the center of the church's ministry, [and] ridiculed theology. When the leaders of the church growth movement claim that theology gets in the way of growth and insist that it does not matter what a particular church believes, they are displaying their debt to Finney. *When leaders of the Vineyard movement praise this sub-Christian enterprise and the barking, roaring, screaming, laughing, and other strange phenomena on the basis that "it works" and one must judge the truth by its fruit, they are following Finney.*

Thus, in Finney's theology, *God is not sovereign; man is not a sinner by nature; the atonement is not a true payment for sin; justification by imputation is insulting to reason and morality; the new birth is simply the result of successful techniques, and revival is a natural result of clever campaigns.*

The influence he exercised and continues to exercise to this day is pervasive. Not only did the revivalist abandon the material principle of the Reformation (justification), he repudiated doctrines, such as original sin and the substitutionary atonement. *Therefore, Finney is not merely an Arminian, but a Pelagian. He is not only an enemy of evangelical Protestantism, but of historic Christianity.* (All quotes are from Charles G. Finney, *Finney's Systematic Theology*, Bethany, 1976).[1] *

Finney believed that a person loses his salvation when he sins. Finney denied the doctrine of original sin, following the fifth century heretic Pelagius. Thus, Finney did not believe that man has a

---

* Emphasis and explanation in this quotation by Dr. Horton was given by the authors.

sinful nature. Finney did not believe that Christ died for our sins.
He believed that Christ's death merely saves us by example. He
did not believe Christ died for our sins in any real sense. Finney
did not believe that the new birth is brought about by the Holy
Spirit. Finney did not believe in justification by faith in Jesus alone.
Finney did not believe in the imputed righteousness of Christ.
Finney believed that justification comes only by "obedience to the
end of life." For Finney, "man is not a sinner by nature; the atonement is not a payment for sin; justification by imputation is false;
the new birth is simply the result of successful techniques, and
revival is the natural result of clever campaigns."[2]

Finney's Testimony

Now we will examine the "salvation" testimony of the man who
held so many false, unscriptural doctrines. Here is Finney's printed
"conversion" experience, given in his own words:

> But after this distinct revelation had stood for some little time be-
> fore my mind, the question seemed to be put, "Will you accept it,
> now, to-day?" I replied, "Yes, I will accept it to-day, or I will die in
> the attempt." . . . As I turned to go up into the woods, I recollect to
> have said, "I will give my heart to God, or I will never come down
> from there." I recollect repeating this as I went up—"I will give my
> heart to God before I ever come down again." . . . Just at that point
> this passage of Scripture seemed to drop into my mind with a flood
> of light: "Then shall ye go and pray unto me, and I will harken unto
> you. Then shall ye seek me and find me, when ye shall search for
> me with all your heart." I instantly seized hold of this with my
> heart. I had intellectually believed the Bible before; but never had
> the truth been in my mind that faith was a voluntary trust instead
> of an intellectual state. I was as conscious as I was of my existence,
> of trusting at that moment in God's veracity. Somehow I knew
> that that was a passage of Scripture, though I do not think I had
> ever read it. I knew that it was God's word, and God's voice, as it
> were, that spoke to me. I cried to Him, "Lord, I take thee at thy

word. Now thou knowest that I do search for thee with all my heart, and that I have come here to pray to thee; and thou hast promised to hear me." That seemed to settle the question that I could, then that day, perform my vow. The Spirit seemed to lay stress upon that idea in the text, "When you search for me with all your heart." The question of when, that is of the present time, seemed to fall heavily into my heart. I told the Lord that I should take him at his word; that he could not lie; and that therefore I was sure that he heard my prayer, and that he would be found of me.[3]

Notice several things about this testimony. On the day he claims salvation, a number of things are missing from Finney's testimony. First, there is no clear word about Jesus Christ in his account. He never mentions the mediatorial work of Christ. In fact, he never mentions Jesus at all! Second, there is no mention of sin. Third, there is no mention of the blood of Jesus. Fourth, there is no mention of the Gospel of Christ (cf. 1 Corinthians 15:1–4). Perhaps a person could trust Jesus and not mention the four points above in his testimony. However, it seems to me that he would say at least a *little* more about what Jesus *did* for him. *Surely Finney should have mentioned that Jesus forgave his sins in his testimony.*

Writing for Spurgeon in the May 1876 *Sword and the Trowel,* V. J. Charlesworth said:

> *We are not surprised that, holding the views he did, Mr. Finney should write his life story with so little reference to the person and work of the Lord Jesus Christ; and that love to a personal Saviour as the constraining motive of Christian obedience should be so conspicuous by its absence.[4]*

Charlesworth makes an astute observation here. One of the things you will notice, as you read Finney's memoirs, is how little he speaks of Jesus' forgiveness, and *how little he speaks of Jesus at all!*

Dr. J. Stanley Mattson has written this regarding Finney's "conversion":

What was wholly new in terms of late eighteenth and nineteenth century New England experience, however, was the idea of salvation as "an offer of something to be accepted" . . . which required nothing more than a willing receiver. . . . *At the moment of his conversion young Finney began forging the outlines of a theology of conversion and revivalism which would endure to the present day.*[5]

Finney's "conversion" contained wrong ideas, and so, his theology was also wrong. As Mattson says, his false ideas continue "to the present day."[6] Thus, Charles Finney's "testimony" has four missing elements:

1. No mention of sin (1 Timothy 1:15).
2. No mention of the mediatorial work of Jesus Christ (1 Timothy 2:5; John 14:6).
3. No mention of the blood of Jesus washing sins away (1 John 1:7).
4. No mention of the Gospel of Christ (1 Corinthians 15:1–4).

Astounding, isn't it? Could this be the reason so many of our churches are morally and spiritually bankrupt today? Could our low spiritual condition be at least partly due to the fact that so much of our religion is rooted in the teachings of a man with such a questionable testimony, a man who believed so many wrong ideas about salvation?

We believe that many problems in evangelicalism today can be traced to the apparently unconverted heart of Charles G. Finney, the man who denied the blood atonement of Christ, did not believe that man has a sinful nature, and taught that the new birth is a product of man's own choice, rather than the work of the Holy Spirit.

This apparently unconverted man has poisoned evangelical religion. His false doctrines have not helped preachers add real converts to their churches. We think that his false doctrine of decisionism has so angered a holy God that He has not sent a major regional revival for over ninety years.

It is our view that unless Finney's idea that man is saved by a decision is given up, there will never be another great classical and biblical revival. The perfidious, Hell-inspired, demonic doctrine that a man is saved by making a decision must, in our judgment, be repudiated, banned, and blasted before a holy God will ever again bless the churches in our land with true revival.

Now let us examine Finney's alleged conversion. First, he says: "The question seemed to be put, 'Will you accept it now, to-day?' I replied, 'Yes, I will accept it to-day, or I will die in the attempt.'" Notice that he said, "I will accept 'it'" instead of "I will accept Jesus" or "I will accept Him." This is doctrinal belief, the idea that you accept a doctrine ("it") rather than accepting the person, Jesus Christ. This is the form of Finneyism into which Zane Hodges and Charles Ryrie seem to fall. The idea that man is saved by believing doctrines (i.e. Charles Ryrie,[7] Zane Hodges,[8]) is exemplified in this early part of Finney's false "testimony." But no one is saved by believing a doctrine, even if it is a true doctrine. We are only saved by believing in Jesus, *Himself*, not by believing things *about* Jesus. A man who has merely believed things *about* Jesus is still a lost man on his way to Hell.

Second, Finney says: "Lord, I take thee at thy word. Thou knowest that I do search for thee with all my heart. . . . That seemed to settle the question that I could then, that day, perform my vow." So Finney adds making a "vow" to doctrinal belief. But no one is saved by making a vow. This is similar to Roman Catholicism. This is Lordship salvation, similar to what John MacArthur teaches. That is why one leading evangelical called MacArthur's Lordship Salvation "the road back to Rome." He said this because the Roman Catholic Church has always preached salvation through Lordship decisions and "vows," rather than through personal faith, which takes the lost sinner directly to Jesus for cleansing in His Blood. That is our glorious, Biblical, Protestant and Baptist Gospel of grace! MacArthur's "Lordship salvation" is not salvation by grace through Jesus. It is indeed the road back to Rome! That is where decisionism in all its forms takes us, as Chuck Colson and J. I. Packer illustrate in their document, "Evangelicals and Catholics Together."

Decisionism Instead of Conversion

Finney's view of salvation by a decision has been embraced by much of evangelicalism. As Michael Horton pointed out:

> Jerry Falwell calls him "one of my heroes and a hero to many evangelicals, including Billy Graham." I recall wandering through the Billy Graham Center some years ago, observing the place of honor given to Finney in the evangelical tradition . . . as a former Wheaton College president rather glowingly cheered, "Finney lives on!"[9]

The older Biblical view of conversion has been largely forgotten. This is the reason so many are now religious but lost. This is the reason that there is so little revival.

Dr. Asahel Nettleton (1783–1843) was the last major evangelical figure to fully oppose the decisionist measures of Charles G. Finney. Nettleton wrote:

> His [Finney's] friends are certainly labouring to introduce those very measures, which I have ever regarded as ultimately working ruin to our churches, and against which I have always guarded as ruinous to the character of revivals.
>
> The friends of brother Finney are afraid to interfere to correct anything, lest they should do mischief, or be denounced as enemies of revivals. And so the bad must all be defended with the good. This sentiment adopted. *will certainly ruin revivals.**
>
> These evils are destined to be propagated from generation to

---

* Emphasis by Dr. Nettleton.

generation, waxing worse and worse. A generation will arise not knowing that a revival ever did or can exist without all those evils.[10]

Nettleton's words foretold, with piercing accuracy, what the future would hold. Finney's decisionist measures brought about a condition where revival has become nearly impossible because we have quenched the Spirit through the use of his methods and false theology. Today, classical revival is almost unheard of in the Western world as a result.

In our time, as in Dr. Nettleton's day, friends of Finney's decisionism "are afraid to interfere to correct anything, lest they should . . . be denounced as enemies of revivals." Even today, men don't want to stir the pot, or re-evaluate Finney's ideas, which are still so much a part of evangelism. Nettleton said that such fear and unwillingness to correct Finney's decisionism "will certainly ruin revivals."

I must repeat here Nettleton's prediction concerning the growth of Finney's methods, which has continued until the present: "These evils are destined to be propagated from generation to generation, waxing worse and worse."[11]

This prediction, given over one hundred and fifty years ago, has come true. *Finney's decisionist methods changed evangelism, short circuited real conversions, and ultimately stopped revival.* Today we live in the burned out aftermath, our churches either liberal, charismatic, or dead; our people claiming to be born again while missing church, divorcing, dancing, committing adultery, holding false doctrine, and aborting their children. An increasing number of pastors commit adultery, while our youth go wild. All of this is the sordid result of that terrible transition from conversion to decisionism which Asahel Nettleton foretold.

Application

How do we overturn the horrible effects of Finneyism? As a Baptist, I am convinced that the local church is the vehicle through which God promotes His work in the world. Therefore it is within the local church that decisionism must be replaced by true conversions. To clarify true and false conversion, we present this application in outline form.

I. Conversion—the false and the true.

1. *False ideas concerning conversion:*

   a. Conversion is not baptism or church membership. These are human works, something a human being can do. "For by grace are ye saved through faith; and that not of yourselves: it is the gift of God: Not of works, lest any man should boast" (Ephesians 2:8–9).

   b. Conversion is not a "feeling" or emotion. Feelings and emotions are deceptive and can change. Conversion is permanent and cannot be changed. ". . . I give unto them eternal life; and they shall never perish . . ." (John 10:28). "Therefore if any man be in Christ, he is a new creature . . ." (2 Corinthians 5:17). It is foolish to base salvation on the feelings and emotions of a "desperately wicked" heart. "The heart is deceitful above all things, and desperately wicked: who can know it?" (Jeremiah 17:9). "For from within, out of the heart of men, proceed evil thoughts . . ." (Mark 7:21). Man's heart and its "feelings" and emotions are not trustworthy in this matter of conversion.

   c. Conversion is not saying "the sinner's prayer," or "asking for forgiveness." These are human works, something that humans can do. **Conversion is something God does for us.** I was saved without saying any prayer. So were John Wesley and Charles Spurgeon. We simply believed on Jesus. Wesley, Spurgeon, and I all believed in "the finished work of Jesus" years before we were converted. At conversion, we believed in Jesus, **Himself!** This is the only decision or "work" God will accept. "This is the work of God, that ye believe on him whom he hath sent" (John 6:29). "Not by works of righteousness which we have done, but according to his mercy he saved us, by the washing of regeneration, and renewing of the Holy Ghost (Titus 3:5).

d. Conversion is not making Christ Lord of every area of your life. Lost sinners are spiritually dead, and cannot make Jesus Lord of *any* area of their lives, much less *every* area. ". . . Dead in trespasses and sins" (Ephesians 2:1). ". . . By nature the children of wrath . . ." (Ephesians 2:3). ". . . Dead in sins . . ." (Ephesians 2:5).

e. Conversion is not believing certain doctrines about Jesus. Romans 10:9–10 is often misapplied to mean that a person is converted by believing the doctrine that Jesus rose from the dead, or the doctrine that He died for our sins. But verse eleven indicates that conversion itself comes by "believing on him," not things *about* Him. Verse fourteen shows that calling on Him without believing on Him does not bring conversion. Roman Catholics believe *that* He died for us and rose from the dead. But they do not believe "on Him." Instead, they believe on their own works for salvation, much like modern decisionists. No wonder we now have Chuck Colson and J. I. Packer proclaiming "Evangelicals and Catholics Together." Charles H. Spurgeon said, "Alas! he was resting in the *plan*, but he had not believed in the *person*. The plan of salvation is most blessed, but it can avail us nothing unless we personally believe in the Lord Jesus Christ Himself."[12]

f. Conversion is not what is commonly called a decision. Probably the clearest verse on this is John 1:13: "Which were born, not of blood, nor of the will of the flesh, nor of the will of man, but of God."

g. Conversion is not refuted or disproved by the verses most often used to support decisionism. Actually, *decisionists have very few verses to support their position*. Here are a few popular ones answered.

   1. *Joel 3:14.* "Multitudes, multitudes in the valley of decision: for the day of the LORD is near in the valley of decision." This refers to people in the army of the Antichrist.

They are in this valley to be destroyed by God. The decision to destroy them is God's. It is totally false, and a horrible use of hermeneutics,* to apply this to decisions today.

2. **Romans 10:9–14.** "That if thou shalt confess with thy mouth the Lord Jesus, and shalt believe in thine heart that God hath raised him from the dead, thou shalt be saved. For with the heart man believeth unto righteousness; and with the mouth confession is made unto salvation. For the scripture saith, Whosoever believeth on him shall not be ashamed. For there is no difference between the Jew and the Greek: for the same Lord over all is rich unto all that call upon him. For whosoever shall call upon the name of the Lord shall be saved. How then shall they call on him whom they have not believed? and how shall they believe in him of whom they have not heard? and how shall they hear without a preacher?" Dr. John R. Rice answers the wrong use of the passage in his famous tract, *What Must I Do To Be Saved?*, written in 1945. This 1945 statement clears up the decisionist use of Romans 10:9–14. Dr. Rice wrote, "Many people believe that a sinner cannot be saved without a period of prayer, without consciously calling on God. However, the Bible does not say that a sinner must pray in order to be saved. In fact, immediately following the verse in Romans 10:13 is an explanation which shows that calling on God is *an evidence of faith in the heart and that it is really faith which settles the matter* . . . no matter how long one prays, if he does not trust in Christ, he can never be saved. If he trusts in Christ without conscious prayer, then he is saved already. There is just one plan of salvation and just one step a sinner must take to secure it. That step is to believe on the Lord Jesus Christ."[13] Though

---

* Bible interpretation.

Dr. Rice was not always consistent (who is?), we think his 1945 comment, given above, is the correct interpretation of Romans 10:9–14. I was saved without praying at all. I simply believed on Jesus. Calling on Jesus (v. 13) does not save unless there is also union with Him (v. 14). It is the union with Him that saves, not the prayer (Acts 16:31).

3. *Matthew 10:32.* "Whosoever therefore shall confess me before men, him will I confess also before my Father which is in heaven." The context of this verse is persecution (see Matthew 10:28–39). This verse declares that converted people will confess Jesus while being persecuted, but the religious lost will deny Him under persecution, as they did in Nazi Germany, the former U.S.S.R., Red China, and Cuba. The verse does not in any way apply to the act of "coming forward," "making a decision," or "confessing Jesus with your mouth" in the comfort of an evangelistic meeting. It just isn't in this verse.

2. *True ideas concerning conversion*

   a. Conversion is a miracle. Since it is a miracle, it is something **God does** for us, not something **we do** by baptism, church membership, a feeling, Lordship commitment, a sinner's prayer, doctrinal belief, or any other work except believing **on** Jesus. ". . . This is the work of God, that ye believe on him whom he hath sent" (John 6:29). "But as many as received him, to them gave he power to become the sons of God . . ." (John 1:12). ". . . Whose heart the Lord opened . . . " (Acts 16:14). "Even when we were dead in sins, hath quickened us together with Christ, (by grace ye are saved)" (Ephesians 2:5). "And you, being dead in your sins, and the uncircimcision of your flesh, hath he quickened together with him, having forgiven you all trespasses" (Colossians 2:13).

   b. Conversion is instantaneous. It does not occur through a process or over a period of time. There is usually a period (sometimes long, sometimes short) in which a person hears the Gospel and thinks about it, but conversion *itself* always happens instantly, in a short period of time. This is true of *every* conversion reported in the Bible, from the conversion of the thief on the cross (Luke 23:39–43) to the conversion of the apostle Paul (Acts 26:9–18). All conversions in the Bible happened in a few moments of time, such as those converted at Pentecost (Acts 2:37–41).

c. Conversion comes by believing "into" and "on" Jesus. "That whosoever believeth *in* him should not perish, but have eternal life" (John 3:15). The Greek word for "in" is *eis*. Zodhiates says of this word: "The primary idea of motion *into* any place or thing . . . meaning 'into.'"[14] "Believe *on* the Lord Jesus Christ, and thou shalt be saved" (Acts 16:31). Here the Greek word for "on" is *epi*. Zodhiates gives us the meaning: "On or upon—to rest upon."[15] So, biblical conversion comes in only one way: by believing "into" Jesus, in other words, to believe "on" Jesus. These concepts are given repeatedly in our old hymns by major hymn-writers like William Cowper, Charlotte Elliott, Charles Wesley, and countless others.

> Rock of ages, cleft for me,
> Let me hide myself *in Thee*.
> Just as I am, without one plea,
> But that Thy blood was shed for me,
> And that Thou biddst me come *to Thee*,
> O Lamb of God, I come, I come.
> Out of my bondage, sorrow, and night,
> Jesus, I come *to Thee*.

A person must actually come *to* the resurrected Jesus and trust in *Him alone* to be saved (Acts 16:31). Nothing else will result in the salvation of a human being:

We have heard the joyful sound,
Jesus saves! Jesus saves!
Spread the tidings all around,
Jesus saves! Jesus saves!

Baptism, church membership, a feeling, Lordship commitment, a sinner's prayer, belief in doctrines, or a decision (other than a decision to believe *on* Jesus, Himself) will *not* save. Lordship commitment only makes the problem greater. ". . . Salvation is of the LORD" (Jonah 2:9). "But to him that worketh not, but believeth on him that justifieth the ungodly, his faith is counted for righteousness" (Romans 4:5). As C. H. Spurgeon said, "Jesus invites all those who labour and are heavy laden to come to Him, and He will give them rest. He does not promise this to those merely dreaming about Him. They must *come*; and they must come *to Him*, and not merely to the church, to baptism, or to the orthodox faith, or to anything short of His divine person."[16]

II. Remedies for decisionism—incorrect and correct.

1. Incorrect remedies for decisionism:

a. Some have felt that fully embracing Reformed theology will of itself cure decisionism. This notion has been proven false by the fact that many Reformed churches are filled with people who base their salvation on some form of decisionism, usually doctrinal belief or Lordship salvation. The very fact that many Reformed churches are all full of decisionists of these forms proves that shifting one's doctrine *alone* does *not* cure decisionism.

b. Giving up the public invitation. Some have felt that doing away with the invitation will cure decisionism. But most often it has not cured this problem in their own churches, where many of their people cling to various decisionist ideas, even though no public invitation is given. Several large churches in the Los Angeles area are all full of decisionism, though a public invitation is never given. It is not the form of the invitation alone that nurtures decisionism, but rather what is said in private to the inquiring soul. *What is done and said during the invitation, and especially after-wards, either leads to decisionism or to Jesus.*

c. Lordship salvation. Adding a "Lordship" commitment to the Gospel (1 Corinthians 15:1–4) has been seen as a cure for decisionism. But adding another human work to the Gospel only makes the problem of decisionism worse. *This error cannot be overcome by adding even more human works!* Lordship commitment can only come *after* the moment of conversion, as a result of it, otherwise salvation is by works rather than solely and completely by believing on Jesus (Acts 16:31).

d. Giving up the sinner's prayer. Merely giving up this prayer does not cure decisionism. But, when using this prayer, the pastor must make sure that the inquirer is trusting Jesus, not the prayer itself, for salvation. A form of this prayer is used with every inquirer in our church. We have them pray, "Jesus, I come to you. Wash away my sins with your Blood. Amen." That's *all* we have them pray.

2. *Correct remedies for decisionism:*

a. Reinstate close personal work. Spurgeon, following the old Baptist method, spent many hours every week alone, deal-ing personally with the lost. He interviewed each and every applicant for baptism, and dealt further with those who were not converted. (See p. 118 in this book for an outline of Spurgeon's method.) This is a wise practice, done by Jesus Himself (John 4:6–30; note verse 30 especially). Paul also practiced this kind of personal method (Acts 16:32). *How can pastors today do the work of Jesus or Paul without following the example of Jesus and Paul? Pastors them-selves must spend much time personally with the lost.*

b. Point the unconverted person to Jesus Himself. Make sure that he understands that Jesus is *not* a spirit, but has a res-urrected flesh and bone body (Luke 24:36–40). This is crucial in our time of New Age and charismatic confusion. Explain exactly *where* Jesus is—at the right hand of God in Heaven, not here on earth (Mark 16:19; Colossians 3:1; 1 Peter 3:22; Romans 8:34). People will not be saved by "trusting" a ghostly charismatic or New Age spirit-Christ who lives in the backyard or in their unconverted heart. Point the lost person to the *real* Jesus where He really *is*! I remained in a lost state for seven years after being baptized in a Southern Baptist church simply because no one ever pointed me to the resurrected Jesus, at the right hand of God, whose blood could wash me, and who could save me. "Neither is there salvation in any other: for there is none other name under heaven given among men, whereby we must be saved" (Acts 4:12).

E'er since by faith I saw the stream
Thy flowing wounds supply,
Redeeming love has been my theme,
And shall be till I die.

Footnotes

1. Michael S. Horton, "The Legacy of Charles Finney," from *Modern Reformation* magazine, computer net posting, April 1, 1996.
2. Ibid.
3. Charles G. Finney, *Autobiography*, pp. 14–17.
4. Vernon J. Charlesworth, *The Sword and the Trowel*, May 1876, p. 218.
5. J. Stanley Mattson, "Charles Grandison Finney and the Emerging Tradition of 'New Measure' Revivalism." Ph.D. dissertation, University of North Carolina (Chapel Hill, 1970), p. 191.
6. Ibid., p. 192.
7. Charles C. Ryrie writes, "To believe in Christ for salvation means to have confidence *that* He can remove the guilt of sin and give eternal life. It means to believe *that* He can solve the problem of sin." The word "that" reveals doctrine as the object of faith, not Jesus *Himself*; Charles C. Ryrie, *So Great Salvation* (Wheaton: Victor Books, 1989), p. 119. Dr. Ryrie declares that faith is not merely "assent to facts" (p. 118), but he then spends three pages proving that faith *is* merely assent to, or belief in, certain facts, using different wording and various evasions (Mark 3:11; James 2:19).
8. Zane Hodges, *Grace in Eclipse* (Dallas: Redencion Viva, 1985), pp. 7–8. Dr. Hodges takes the same basic approach as Dr. Ryrie, that saving faith

comes by believing things *about* Jesus, rather than the union with the resurrected Christ in Heaven, a supernatural union, resulting in conversion. Hodges declares "to believe in," and "believe that" "refers to the same act" (p. 7). He says, "To believe in Jesus is to believe something about Him" (p. 8). This is "salvation by doctrinal belief" rather than salvation by coming to, and resting on, Jesus Himself—i.e. union with Christ Himself (cf. John 5:40; John 6:44; Matthew 11:28).

9. Horton, "The Legacy of Charles Finney" (see footnote 1).

10. Asahel Nettleton, quoted in Bennett Tyler and Andrew Bonar, *The Life and Labours of Asahel Nettleton* (Edinburgh: Banner of Truth Trust, 1975, reprinted from the 1854 edition), pp. 347–49.

11. Ibid.

12. Charles H. Spurgeon, *Around the Wicket Gate* (Pasadena, TX: Pilgrim Publications, 1992 reprint), p. 27.

13. John R. Rice, *What Must I Do To Be Saved?* (Sword of the Lord, 1945), pp. 16–17.

14. Spiros Zodhiates, Th.D., *The Complete Word Study Dictionary of the New Testament* (Chattanooga: AMG Publishers, 1992), p. 521.

15. Ibid, p. 618.

16. Spurgeon, *Around the Wicket Gate*, pp. 29–30.

Chapter Seven

Real Conversion

For the time will come when they will not endure sound doctrine; but after their own lusts shall they heap to themselves teachers, having itching ears; And they shall turn away their ears from the truth, and shall be turned unto fables. But watch thou in all things, endure afflictions, do the work of an evangelist. . . .

—II Timothy 4:3–5

Chapter two of this book began with a quotation from Asahel Nettleton, the American evangelist who opposed Finney's decisionist techniques. This statement could almost be seen as a prophecy concerning the evil effects of decisionism:

These evils are destined to be propagaged from generation to generation, waxing worse and worse.

—Asahel Nettleton ,1854 edition of
The Life and Labours of Asahel Nettleton

Here are the main points we have covered so far in this book:

1. Our culture is unravelling, with no end in sight.
2. Decisionism has failed to cure the problem.
3. Stronger preaching against sin is needed.
4. Careful counselling by the pastor should be done in a quiet place. There should usually be more than one such counsel-

ling session, perhaps many in certain cases, but at least a few in all cases.

Imagine yourself going to a doctor's office with a bleeding sore on your face. In the office are a number of people with crutches, some in wheelchairs, others wheezing, barely able to breathe. You are all waiting to see the doctor. After a few minutes, a nurse runs in and gives everyone in the room a red pill. Then she smiles brightly and says, "You're all cured! Go home!"

"But, but," you protest, "we have different symptoms."

"Oh, that's all right," the nurse answers, "One prescription fits everyone."

"But I wanted to see the doctor," you protest.

"Oh, he never sees anyone who is sick," she answers. "He delegates that to me."

As she turns to go, she says, "Come back when you're well. The doctor will be glad to see you then."

Sadly, many churches handle lost inquirers about like that. *If medical doctors treated patients in their offices like many pastors treat inquirers in their churches, they would constantly be faced with malpractice suits.*

Rev. F. L. Chapell warned that our churches would fill up with lost people unless pastors made sure they are converted: "The dark days that preceded the Great Awakening will come again unless somebody stands firmly and clearly and decidedly by the doctrine of a converted church-membership."[1]

The tragic situation in our churches today could easily be reversed by following Spurgeon's advice to preachers:

> If you wish to see results from your sermons you must be accessible to inquirers. . . . You should appoint frequent and regular seasons for seeing all who are seeking after Christ, and you should cordially invite such to come and speak with you.[2]

Spurgeon's advice echos that given by Richard Baxter in the seventeenth century:

The work of conversion is the first and great thing we must drive at; after this we must labour with all our might. . . . We must be ready to give advice to inquirers, who come to us. A minister is not to be merely a public preacher, but to be known as a counsellor for their souls, as the physician is for their bodies. . . . To this end it is very necessary that you be well acquainted with practical cases, and especially that you be acquainted with the nature of saving grace, and be able to assist them in trying their state, and in resolving the main question that concerns their everlasting life or death. One word of seasonable, prudent advice, given by a minister to persons in necessity, may be of more help than many sermons.[3]

These two men from the past strongly urge us to love the lost enough to spend time with them and help them.

Evangelistic Preaching

The kind of counselling we are suggesting will be of little help unless it comes after evangelistic preaching. By this we mean preaching which does two things:

1. Exposes sin by the Law, showing the sinner that he is lost and helpless (Galatians 3:24) by appealing to his conscience.
2. Extolls the virtues of the Gospel: i.e. the death, burial, and resurrection of Christ (1 Corinthians 15:1–4) as the only remedy for sin.

There is a great need for preaching on the evilness of sin today. As Dr. J. Gresham Machen so aptly put it, "Without the consciousness of sin, the whole of the gospel will seem to be an idle tale."[4] There is a great need for preaching on the wrath of God as well.

By this, we do not mean verse-by-verse teaching or preaching *about* certain doctrines (which depersonalizes them—always a trap).We are talking about preaching to the people in front of you on their sin, on Hell, on the wrath of God.

Duncan Campbell saw the need for preaching on sin and judgment back in the 1940s and 1950s:

Duncan Campbell was often criticized for declaring the wrath of God night after night, but he saw this only as a backcloth to the gospel.[5] Campbell's method was to preach on sin, condemnation and hell during the services.[6]

It should be remembered that the last great regional revival in the Western world occurred under Duncan Campbell's preaching.[7] Oh, for God to send such preachers again, at this hour!

Focus on These Great Baptist and Protestant Themes
Evangelistic preaching, to be effective, *must focus on these great Baptist and Protestant themes:*

- The *self-examination of the heart* (Have you preached to the people in your church on the need to examine themselves to see whether they are in the faith? 2 Corinthians 13:5)
- The *depravity of man* (Have you preached to the people in your church on their depravity lately? Ephesians 2:1, 2, 5).
- The *atonement of Jesus* (Have you preached to the people in your church on the atonement of Jesus for their sins lately? Romans 5:6–9; 1 Corinthians 15:3).
- The *last judgment* (Have you preached to the people in your church on what will happen to them at the last judgment lately? Revelation 20:11–15)
- The *unpardonable sin* (Have you preached to the people in your church on the unpardonable sin lately? Matthew 12:31–32)
- The *reprobation of sinners* (Have you preached to the people in your church on the reprobation of sinners lately? Romans 1:24–28)
- The *fire of Hell* (Have you told the unconverted people in your church that they are going to burn forever in Hell lately? Matthew 5:46; Luke 16:19–31)
- The *Ten Commandments* (Have you preached to the people in your church on the fact that they have broken the Ten Com-

mandments lately? Exodus 20:3–17; 1 John 3:4)

- The *blood of Jesus* (Have you preached to the people in your church on the blood of Jesus lately? Strangely, some Bible preachers are suddenly unsure of the blood in our day. There will be no revival without great blood sermons. If there is no blood in Heaven, then you will never get in there! Hebrews 9:7; 10:19)

- The *resurrection of Jesus* (Have you preached to the people in your church on the physical resurrection of Jesus lately, or do you reserve this subject for Easter only? Remember, "If Christ be not raised, your faith is vain [empty]; . . . ye are yet in your sins"—1 Corinthians 15:17. Remember also that ". . . we shall be saved by his life"—Romans 5:10. Sermons on this subject are especially important in a day of charismatism and New Age mysticism.)

- The *absolute necessity of regeneration* (Have you preached to the people in your church on their need of regeneration recently? John 3:3, 7; Titus 3:5)

These great themes should constantly appear as the subjects of evangelistic sermons, if we wish to see conversions, and if we truly desire revival.

Asahel Nettleton pointed out that these doctrines were preached by the apostles and that:

> With these, idol temples were demolished—sinners pricked in their hearts, and brought to bow submissively to the Saviour's feet. These are the doctrines which were preached in the time of the glorious reformation from papacy, throughout the whole Protestant world. These were the weapons used by Luther, Melancthon, Calvin, Cranmer, and Knox. They went forth with the sword of the Spirit pressing the consciences of men. . . .
>
> These too are the doctrines which have been preached in the late revivals, in New England. Doctrines which have awakened the enmity of thousands, and have shown sinners their opposition to

God. Doctrines which many have opposed with all their hearts, in which contest thousands have been convicted and slain. These are the weapons which have been wielded by the hand of the divine Spirit and have been mighty through God to the pulling down of strong holds. These are the doctrines which thousands have embraced, by their own confession, at the very time when they submitted to God. . . .[8]

Oh, for God to send Spirit-anointed preachers to take up these grand old themes of our Baptist and Protestant forebears, and proclaim them up and down the land without fear of the lost evangelicals seated in the pews in front of them!

The kind of counselling which follows will do little good unless it is preceded by hard, sin-condemning, conscience-probing, Christ-exalting evangelistic preaching. Dr. John R. Rice* said:

In the very nature of the case, people do not repent of their sins until they are conscious and convicted of their sins. Jesus said, "They that be whole need not a physician, but they that are sick." Until a man knows he is sick, he does not feel the need of a physician. A preacher friend said, "You have to get people lost before you can get them saved." . . . Why would a sinner want Christ if he were not conscious of his sin, did not feel the need of a Saviour?[9]

Sin Confronted in the Pastor's Study

When the sermon is over, lost people are invited to my office. They sit there quietly reading the following material. They read this be-

---

* We agree with Dr. Rice on the subject of preaching against sin. We disagree with him on the subject of Charles G. Finney's decisionist techniques and on some related issues. But many of Dr. Rice's sermons are evangelistic classics, such as "The Unpardonable Sin," "All Satan's Apples Have Worms," "Neglect, the Shortest Way to Hell," "Missing God's Last Train for Heaven," "God's Slaughter Crew," "The Scarlet Sin," "Religious But Lost," and many others. Preachers should obtain and read these powerful, conscience-probing sermons. It would do many churches good if pastors preached these sermons by Dr. Rice to their people. I have done just that on several occasions, always giving full credit to Rice before preaching.

fore Dr. Cagan or I see them. The following pages are a reproduction of what we give to the people when they come to my office after the sermon:

YOUR BIGGEST PROBLEM—SIN

Dear Friend:

I am glad you came here today. I hope you came because you are thinking about your *sins*. Your *sins* are many and they are terrible in God's sight.

1. Your *sins* have separated you from God: "Your iniquities [sins] have separated between you and your God, and your sins have hid his face from you . . ." (Isaiah 59:2).

2. Your *sins* are all known by God: "The eyes of the LORD are in every place, beholding the evil . . ." (Proverbs 15:3a). God knows every *sin* you have ever committed.

3. Your *sins* are recorded in God's books in Heaven: ". . . The dead were judged out of those things which were written in the books, according to their works" (Revelation 20:12b). Every *sin* you have ever committed was seen by God and has been written down in these books in Heaven. You are in trouble!

4. At the last judgment, you will stand before God, and He will read your *sins* out of His books. Your *sins* will condemn you: ". . . Be sure your sin will find you out" (Numbers 32:23b).

5. Even your *sins* which you kept secret will be read from the books by God at the last judgment: "For God shall bring every work into judgment, with every secret thing . . ." (Ecclesiastes 12:14).

6. Sinful *words* which you have said will be read out of the books by God, and your *sinful* words will condemn you: "For by thy words . . . thou shalt be condemned" (Matthew 12:37).

7. Your *sinful* thoughts will be read out of God's books. *Sins* you have thought about will condemn you. "And God saw . . . that every imagination of the thoughts of his heart was only evil" (Genesis 6:5).

8. You have *sinned* by missing church. This shows you have

broken the first commandment given by Jesus in Matthew 22:37–38. This is a terrible *sin*: "Thou shalt love the Lord thy God with all thy heart, and with all thy soul, and with all thy mind. This is the first and great commandment" (Matthew 22:37–38). Each time you miss church, this *sin* of not loving God as you should is recorded in God's books. You are in trouble because of your *sins*. This *sin* alone is enough to condemn you.

9. You have committed at least one of the following *sins*:

- *Pride*
- *Cursing*
- *Greed*
- *Rejecting Jesus*
- *False religion*
- *Hatred and anger*
- *Selfishness*
- *Talking back to parents*
- *Lying*
- *Sex sin*
- *Pornography*
- *Stealing*
- *Drugs or alcohol-*
- *Not loving God as much as you should*
- *Missing church*

Sin is the transgression (or breaking) of the law (1 John 3:4).

10. You have committed at least one of these horrible *sins*. Your *sins* are written down in God's books in Heaven.

Even if you could stop *sinning* now, it would *not* help you. If you never again committed even one *sin*, it is *too late* for you. The *sins* you have already done are written in God's books. These *sins* of yours are enough already to condemn you. *IT IS TOO LATE FOR YOU TO BE GOOD.*

Even if you are sorry for your *sins* it will not help you. Your sorrow will not remove your *sins* from God's books. *IT IS TOO LATE FOR YOU TO BE SORRY FOR YOUR SINS.*

Nothing you can do can get rid of your sins! No one but Jesus *can take your **sins** out of God's books.*

*No one can remove your **sins** but **Jesus**—by His blood. He was crucified to pay the penalty for your sins.*

*No one but Jesus has "power on earth to forgive **sins**"* (Matthew 9:6).

*Do you want **Jesus** to forgive your **sins** and remove them from God's books?*

*Will you come to **Jesus** so He can wash your **sins** away with His blood?*

*Jesus is **not** angry with you. He loves you.*

Jesus is alive. He is seated at the right hand of God in Heaven.

An Outline on Counselling

C. H. Spurgeon strongly urged every Baptist preacher to have a quiet room where he could talk at length with the lost. He told the students at his Pastor's College:

> It is shocking to think that there are ministers who have no method whatever for meeting the anxious. From the very first you should appoint frequent and regular seasons for seeing all who are seeking after Christ, and you should cordially invite such to come and speak with you. Seek out the wandering sheep one by one, do not grudge your labour, for your Lord in His parable represented the good shepherd as bringing home his sheep, not in a flock, but one at a time.[10]

Speaking on the same subject, the seventeenth century preacher Richard Baxter said:

> The work of conversion is the first and great thing we must drive at; after this we must labour with all our might. . . . We must be ready to give advice to inquirers, who come to us. A minister is not to be merely a public preacher, but to be known as a counsellor for their souls, as the physician is for their bodies.[11]

These two men from the past strongly urge us to love the lost enough to spend time with them and help them. This manual on conversion is given to help pastors in the counselling work which Spurgeon and Baxter described. We do not believe that people are saved through our methods alone. Anyone who comes to Jesus is saved (John 6:37). But we believe that the following manual can be helpful in making sure inquiring souls actually do come to Him.

Are We Overreacting?

A copy of this manuscript was sent to a lady to be reviewed. She is a very intelligent person with a seminary degree from a world-famous school. The manuscript came back from her with a comment that the first part of this book is insightful, but that we have "overreacted" in this final section, on counselling the lost.

We thought about that for several days. Then it dawned on Dr. Hymers that this lady is the wife of a pastor! Of course she would think we have overreacted! *If we are right, then her own husband is wrong, because he doesn't use the methods we give here!*

Before you conclude that this section is too detailed or too lengthy, please, dear reader, at least consider the possibility that we may have rediscovered something you need to know. Please be open to that possibility. Try to look at the subject of counselling the unconverted through new eyes, as though you had never thought of it before. That way you will be less likely to close your mind, and emotionally reject what we say based on your own personal experience.

Remember, we are not giving a quick, untested answer to decisionism. Both of us are seminary graduates with earned doctorates. Dr. Cagan has twenty years of experience in the ministry. Dr. Hymers has forty years of experience. The ideas on counselling which you are about to read have been tested in our own church for many years. *So, please, evaluate this section with great care.* Don't simply reject our ideas with a knee-jerk emotional reaction.

What Is Conversion?

A. We must have in mind a definition of salvation through Christ.

Conversion gives a man a new nature and standing before God and, thus, produces a new direction in his life. Conversion is the result of that work of the Holy Spirit which draws a lost sinner to Jesus Christ for justification and regeneration, and changes the sinner's standing before God from lost to saved, imparting divine life to the depraved soul, thus producing a new direction in the life of the convert. The objective side of salvation is justification. The subjective side of salvation is regeneration. The result is conversion.

1. *Historically:* "For I delivered unto you first of all that which I also received, how that Christ died for our sins according to the scriptures; And that he was buried, and that he rose again the third day according to the scriptures" (1 Corinthians 15:3–4).

2. *Personally:* ". . . Believe on the Lord Jesus Christ, and thou shalt be saved . . ." (Acts 16:31). As Spurgeon said, "That faith which saves the soul is believing on a person, depending upon Jesus for eternal life."[12]

3. The act of believing on Christ (also called trusting Christ) is the means by which the atonement historically given for all mankind is received by the individual sinner and applied to him. Christ died for all men and women, yet not all are saved, because most people do not trust Him.

4. This act of believing on Christ or trusting Him is no mere agreement to the historical facts of the Gospel. It is instead an act in which the sinner trusts in Christ the person, Christ Himself (John 1:12). A. T. Pierson was quoted by H. C. Thiessen in his *Lectures in Systematic Theology.* Dr. Pierson wrote: "Here, then, is the starting point for any who would exercise saving faith; he must **receive** Jesus as Savior, Christ, Son of God; not simply the witness God gave concerning His Son, but the Son of God **Himself.**"[13] Or, as C. H. Spurgeon put it, "The mere knowledge of these facts will not, however, save

us, unless we really and truly trust our souls in the Redeemer's hands."[14]

5. This act is unique among all the things that a human being does. Although called a "work" in John 6:29, it is in a class of its own and is distinguished from all human works, such as going to church, giving up sins, witnessing, fasting, giving money, praying, rededicating your life, and so on. Believing on Jesus is the *only* "work" or "decision" that will save a person (John 6:29). The act of trusting Christ is actually supernatural:

   a. It reaches from earth to heaven, going outside of a person and even outside of this earthly universe. While a sinner can of his own power give up sins, pray, come to church, read the Bible, and so on, he cannot perform either aspect of salvation: he cannot pay for his own sins (1 Corinthians 15:3–4) and he cannot of his own abilities, without the grace of God, come to Christ (John 6:44), who is in Heaven (Mark 16:19; Colossians 3:1; 1 Peter 3:22). Thus, it would be impossible for a person to come to, trust, or otherwise contact Jesus, if it depended upon purely human faculties: but Jesus as the omnipresent Son of God is actually "standing at the door and knocking" (see Revelation 3:20) and the grace of God actually makes saving trust possible (Ephesians 2:8–9). How wonderful is the love of God!

   b. Furthermore, the sinner in his depraved state cannot be saved, and does not even want to be saved. He is ". . . dead in trespasses and sins . . ." (Ephesians 2:1) with the ". . . understanding darkened . . ." (Ephesians 4:18). It is only God that awakens a sinner and places within him both a desire to come to Christ and the ability to do so (John 6:44).

   Were it not for the grace of God, no lost sinner could or would trust in Christ, or even want to. But God's love is so marvellous and so great that not only did Christ die for us (Rom. 5:8), but God draws each person (through prevenient grace) at least once in his life and makes it possible for him to trust Christ (Titus 2:11) if he chooses. ". . . He first loved us" (1 John 4:19).

Herein is love, not that we loved God (we did not), but that he loved us (first), and sent his Son to be the propitiation for our sins (1 John 4:10).

6. When a person trusts Christ, he receives (whether he feels it or even knows it) all the benefits associated with Christ: forgiveness of sins, the new birth, and many other benefits. Christ Himself thus takes priority over all the results that go along with trusting Him: joy, peace, assurance, a new life, and even the new birth. If a person comes to Christ, he receives all the benefits of Christ thrown in (1 Corinthians 1:30–31).

7. The act of trusting Christ or believing on Christ or coming to Christ is the goal to be sought. The lost sinner must seek to trust Christ, and the pastor or personal worker must speak to the lost sinner with the intention of motivating him to trust Christ (Acts 8:30–37; Romans 10:14).

B. There are many errors regarding salvation, declaring that it is not through Christ.

1. Salvation not necessary at all, with a person's "life-interest" or "life-trust" somewhere else: money, friends, family, knowledge, sex, self, etc. Often combined with a denial of Christian doctrine openly or practically; the person may think the Bible isn't true, deny the existence of Hell, think there is no after-life, and so on.

2. Salvation necessary, but obtained without Christ; by works, holiness, study, attendance at meetings, religiosity, abstaining from sins, prayer, confession, and so on (e.g. Judaism, Islam, etc.).

3. Salvation allegedly by Christ, but in fact Christ is subjected to or "piped through" something else.

   a. Catholic: Christ is mediated through baptism, communion, confession, church attendance, etc. (Worse: salvation through saints or the virgin; Christ distant.)

b. Evangelical: Christ is obtained or mediated through a sinner's prayer (without saving faith in Jesus), doctrinal belief, study, church attendance, or something else; doing one of these things confers Christ or proves that a person has Him.

c. Pentecostal: Christ is obtained/mediated through experiences, tongues, good feelings, life going well, etc.

These errors are *ontologically* wrong; that is, they put Christ under or "pipe Him through" something less than Himself, such as church attendance, the mass, the sinner's prayer, or doctrine. In fact, we are saved by a *direct* trust in Christ, who is greater than these other things: "And he is before all things, and by him all things consist" (Colossians 1:17).

C. All of these errors come short of actually trusting Christ, although His name may be used.

Just as a Catholic who names Jesus but in fact trusts baptism is not saved, in the same way an evangelical who names the name of Jesus but in fact trusts the sinner's prayer or doctrinal belief instead of trusting Christ, Himself, is not saved. This explains why many professing "born again" believers have no real Christian life, live in habitual gross sin, and in general give no evidence of union with Christ—simply because they have in fact not trusted Christ, not rested in Him, not entered into a saving union with Him (John 5:40; John 6:40).

The pastor is to guide the lost person toward a salvation experience through trusting Christ, just as Evangelist did in *Pilgrim's Progress*.

This *may* happen while a person prays a sinner's prayer, but does *not* happen *because* he prays the prayer. The key element is trusting Christ, not the prayer. John R. Rice wrote that a person can be saved without prayer in his tract "What Must I Do to be Saved?" Charles Spurgeon, John Wesley, and Dr. Hymers were all saved without saying a "sinner's prayer," by a simple act of faith in Jesus Himself (John 3:18). These men did not pray when they were saved, they simply put the trust of their hearts in Jesus. "With the heart man believeth unto righteousness" (Romans 10:10).

Two Sides of Salvation
A. The subjective side of salvation—regeneration (John 3:3; 1 John 3:9).

This is what is called the new birth itself; when the Holy Spirit imparts new life to the person who has trusted Christ. This gives him the power to live the Christian life and the new (divine) nature. This new life reflects itself in the convert (1 Corinthians 6:11).

B. The objective side of salvation—justification (Romans 5:1, 6–9, Romans 4:5; Isaiah 53).

This refers to the forgiveness of sins through the shed blood of Christ who died on the cross to pay for sins (Romans 5:8–9). The proper order—justification precedes regeneration. This order places Christ in the most important place, where He should be (the order is logical rather than chronological, since both happen in an instant when a person trusts Christ).

C. The result—conversion.
1. A person who turns to Christ and trusts Him (believes on Him, unites with Him, comes to Him) for forgiveness (justification) is objectively justified and subjectively receives the new birth (Romans 4:5). As a result, he is converted (Matthew 18:3).
2. A person who looks to Christ for a mere spiritual "experience," for personal power (even to overcome sin), for feelings, for a change, and so on, will get neither justification nor regeneration (Acts 8:18–23). As a result, he will not be converted.
3. So, we want the inquirer to turn to Christ for the forgiveness of his sins, which are written in God's books in Heaven (e.g. Revelation 20:12–15). These sins will accuse the lost sinner at the judgment even if he no longer commits them, because

they are recorded in Heaven (Revelation 20:12). They can only be forgiven by the blood of Christ (Hebrews 9:14, 22).

Stages of Conversion
A. Introduction: Preliminary considerations

1. The only thing needed to be saved is to trust Christ. Thus, a person does not need to pass through a noticeable or discernable period of awakening or conviction of sin in order to be saved.

   a. Some have been saved without being under conviction of sin at the moment of their conversion such as blind Bartimaeus (Mark 10:47–52), though he was undoubtedly aware of his sinful and miserable state and in that sense was prepared for conversion by prevenient grace.

   b. However, in most cases people *do* need to see their sins at the moment of conversion, or they will not trust Christ. As Dr. J. Gresham Machen wrote: "Without the consciousness of sin, the whole of the gospel will seem to be an idle tale."[15]

   c. Some wish to focus on the details of salvation and "how to" trust Christ, but have no sense of sin, so the entire process is an "idle tale" at best (John 8:44).

   d. Some wish to analyze themselves and seek for a consciousness of sin as an end in itself rather than looking at Christ. This too is fruitless (Ephesians 4:18–19; 1 Timothy 4:2).

2. Trusting Christ is instantaneous.

   a. The "stages" suggested here usually come to pass over time. As Charles Haddon Spurgeon wrote, "There may be such a thing as faith at first sight; but usually we reach faith by stages: we become interested, we consider, we hear evidence, and so are led to believe"[16] (cf. Mark 8:22–25). But the moment of belief is itself instantaneous.

   b. However, these stages can happen quickly and be a logical order rather than an order in time (Acts 8:30–38). The important thing is to lead the person to Christ rather than to make an idol out of a process of awakening and conviction and seek that as though it were the goal itself.

B. The unawakened or careless sinner

Almost everyone who comes for counselling the first time or two is in this state. To be in this state does not mean that a person is not religious, does not have an outwardly clean life, or is not interested in the Bible, the church, or the external things of God. Nicodemus, the apostle Paul, and John the Baptist were unawakened yet religious and clean before their conversions (John 3:10; Acts 26:4-5; Acts 9:5; John 1:31, 33–34). "... I knew him not ..." (John 1:31). "... I knew him not ..." (John 1:33). "... I saw ..." (John 1:34).

This is John the Baptist unconverted and then converted. John is a transitional figure between the old and new dispensations, so this cannot be emphasized too dogmatically. However, the above verses must have deep significance regarding John's own conversion.

It is the pastor's job through the use of the Bible, pleading and reasoning as the human instrument, and by the power of God as the divine instrument, to move the sinner into an awakened and convicted state, and finally to conversion.

Unawakened sinners, whether they are new to the church or whether they have been coming to church for a long time, tend to have these two characteristics:

1. They have preconceived religious opinions about God (the Father), Jesus Christ, salvation (how to get to Heaven), Heaven and Hell, and so on. Unawakened sinners hold to these opinions even though they may have been sitting under Gospel preaching for years. They may outwardly profess orthodox Christianity, but in fact upon examination have an entirely different religion (true of lost but orthodox Christians before the Great Awakening, the 1859 revival, etc.).

These opinions can be acquired at any time in life, usually by attending a church or religious meeting and hearing the Gospel preached.

It is not necessary to attend a church many times in order to form a religious opinion. Many people have formed their opinions by attending a single religious meeting, or even by watching Christian television or by reading a book, or by conversations with others, during which religious opinions are expressed.

a. It is important for the pastor to ask the sinner what was his church or religion in the past. This will give you an idea of how the sinner thinks.

   i. People with a *Catholic background* will generally think in terms of salvation by works: quitting some sins, which they call "repentance," going to church, following Jesus, loving Jesus, confession, and generally being good. They will also often think that Jesus and God the Father are one and the same in every respect, and thus do not really understand how Jesus acts as the mediator between God and men (1 Timothy 2:5).

   ii. People with a *Baptist, evangelical, or Reformed background* will often trust baptism, saying the sinner's prayer, or mentally believing Christian doctrine, such as being able to recite the plan of salvation. They often abuse the doctrine of the security of the believer to the point of thinking that if they have at any time said a prayer, been baptized, joined a church, or believed Christian doctrine, they have therefore been saved and are now merely "backslidden," even though they have never been converted. Rededication is deadly to such a person. If he rededicates his life, he will go to Hell, because salvation and rededication come in two completely different ways.

   iii. People with a *charismatic or Pentecostal background* usually think in terms of feelings and experiences. If a person has had an experience with what he thinks is the

Holy Spirit, feels God's blessing in his life, or feels peace and joy in his heart, etc., he considers himself saved. Many times such people come for counselling seeking assurance or another feeling when in fact they have never been saved by trusting **Christ**.

b. To explore further, the pastor should ask the sinner, "How do you hope to get to Heaven?" This will reveal what the sinner believes about salvation. It will reveal the sinner's false hope about salvation—what the sinner hopes to do, or thinks that he has already done, to get to Heaven.

If the sinner already thinks that he is going to Heaven (should he die then), the pastor should ask him what a person should do to get to Heaven. If the time is short, it is better to ask this rather than to have the sinner repeat what he considers to be his salvation testimony, which is often a long story of the experiences in the person's life, leading up to an abrupt ending, with little or no mention of Jesus forgiving sins by His Blood. Cut past this monologue and simply ask, "What should a person do to get to Heaven? Please tell me in one sentence." This question alone will often reveal whether someone is saved or not, and what their false hope is. It is an eye-opener! It will show you how many lost people attend your church!

What we are looking for is this: has the person come to Jesus? Has he come to Jesus because he could not get rid of his sins in any other way? Is he justified through union with the Son of God?

c. It is **very important** for the pastor to find out what the sinner actually **thinks**. Often what the sinner says rather casually is not what he really **thinks**. One person said that he had never been to any church but the Catholic, but continually talked with Pentecostal jargon. I asked him if he had watched or heard any religious teachers on television or radio. It turned out that he had in fact watched so-called Christian television and formed his religious opinions there.

This person was properly counted as a Pentecostal rather than a Catholic. Some people, when asked how they hoped to get to Heaven, answer mechanically, "trust Jesus" or "believe in Jesus," not because they have done so or are about to do so, but because they have heard the words and repeat them back.

For this reason, the pastor must ask, "How do you hope to do that?" or "What do you mean by that (trust Jesus)?" If the sinner continues with other memorized words, repeat the question and ask him not to use the same words twice. Keep going until the sinner answers with what he really thinks.

What the sinner really thinks may be the exact opposite of what his verbal statement says. He may say "trust Jesus," or "rest in Jesus," but upon exploration he means "give every part of your life to Jesus every day," which means to become perfect—and he is unaware of the need of the blood of Jesus to atone for his sins of the past.

Some sinners may say "I don't know," or "just believe in Jesus." Usually they are not honestly seeking the truth, but are trying to push the responsibility for their sins and their lost condition over onto the church, God, Jesus, the pastor, or someone else.

2. Unawakened sinners have no real sense of their *sin.* They may admit to having made mistakes. They often excuse their sins, blaming their own ignorance, their parents, their husbands, or someone else.

They may admit to grievous sins in the past (abortion, drugs, sexual sin, blasphemy, etc.), but are quite detached from them now, since they are not doing them *that day.* But they should be pointed to Revelation 20:12 to explain that their sins remain on God's record in Heaven.

They may admit to sin in a general sense ("We're all sinners." "Nobody's perfect") but do not consider themselves guilty of any major crime. Often, when asked what sins they have committed, they will mention lightly sins like "pride," "missing church," "selfishness," and other so-called "minor imperfections," even though they may be guilty of horrible crimes and sins.

The emotional attitude of unawakened sinners usually reflects their spiritual state. Some will argue with the pastor, defend themselves, answer dryly as though they were in a classroom, or even laugh. The pastor must try to wake the sinner out of his slumber so he will see that he has indeed transgressed against a holy God.

3. It is the pastor's job to try to get the sinner *awakened* so that he (not only with his mouth, but in fact or "in his heart") considers himself to be:

   a. a guilty sinner who has broken God's laws (James 2:10; Romans 3:19–20), his sins being recorded in God's books, and thus righteously deserving of punishment (Revelation 20:12).

   b. a hopeless or *lost* sinner who has no way of his own to be saved (his false hope) and must come to *Christ* to be saved by His mercy. This is in fact what the idea of being "lost" means—not only being a sinner, but of having no way out or no hope (Luke 15:17, 24, 32; John 9:12; Luke 19:10; Matthew 18:11).

   The pastor must thus confront the sinner with his sin and his hopelessness. When a sinner has reached the state of awakening or conviction described here, he will be ready to come to Christ, and usually will do so rather simply (often surprisingly so).

   The art of bringing a sinner to an awakened and convicted state is the work of the Holy Spirit in cooperation with the pastor. It is acquired by experience more than learned in a classroom or academic setting. To win souls requires wisdom (Proverbs 11:30). Above all, it requires grace, help, and power from God, without which the best words of the worker are but empty noise.

C. The awakened/convicted sinner (Ephesians 5:14).

1. The pastor must firmly confront the sinner with the reality and greatness of his sin. ". . . All have sinned, and come short of the glory of God" (Romans 3:23). ". . . The soul that sinneth, it shall die" (Ezekiel 18:4).

   To do this, you must use God's *law*: ". . . By the law is the knowledge of sin" (Romans 3:20). ". . . The law was our schoolmaster to bring us unto Christ, that we might be justified by faith" (Galatians 3:24).

   God's law is the "thou shalt" and "thou shalt not" of the Bible. The best known example of God's laws is the Ten Commandments. Go through the Ten Commandments and show the sinner, one by one, how he has violated God's law and is guilty (Exodus 20:4–17).

   Sin is a rebellion against God. "All we like sheep have gone astray; we have turned every one to his own way . . ." (Isaiah 53:6). ". . . Sin is the transgression [breaking] of the law (1 John 3:4).

   The following describes how a sinner breaks the law and sins:
   a. God says not to do something (lie, have sex outside of marriage, curse, steal, murder) and the sinner *does it*.
   b. God says to do something (honor father and mother, come to church), and the sinner *refuses to do it*.

   The greatest commandment of all is to love the Lord God with all thy heart, soul, and mind (Matthew 22:37). Every lost sinner has broken this greatest of all commandments. The pastor must firmly confront the sinner with his sin. He must ask the sinner, "What is the biggest (or worst) sin you have done?" Some sinners will say they have sinned in general, but are not guilty of anything in particular. Others will lightly mention such "minor" matters as pride, selfishness, or missing church. They may even say they have "rejected Jesus," but by this they do not mean that they are guilty of the greatest sin of all, but rather that they are simply in an "un-born again" state rather than in a born again one, and they are ready to be born again if only someone would show them how; it is really not their fault at all. In this, they have deceived themselves, and need to be shown the truth.

None of these statements should be accepted by the pastor. Instead, try to find the person's "life sin" or "big sin" which keeps him from trusting Christ. (This is often a hatred of or rebellion against father or mother.) Such a sin may have been committed years in the past, but yet remains with the person and stains his life, his soul, and his eternal record before God.

No one is saved by stopping any sin, even the great sins of his life. But there are many people who will not be saved if they do not deal with their sin, if they are not serious about it and have every intention of going on with their sin. Actually, they have an argument with the Bible, with God, and His Word. One person blurted out to me without being asked, "I think there are some things in my life that I have to change, or I can't be a Christian." The person was right.

However, change *alone* will not produce salvation. This is not a "pre-condition" for salvation. It simply means that the sinner must stop clinging to (or resting in) something else before he can rest on Jesus.

For other people, the obstacle may not be a sin but a false idea, such as the thought that their own goodness saves them, a fear that Jesus is angry with them and does not love them, or a false doctrine such as a belief that Jesus is still on the cross, or did not rise from the dead, etc. Experience will teach you how to diagnose each case.

If you cannot find the person's "great sin" in the time available, try to find *a* great sin with which you can confront the sinner. (Something like sexual sin, drugs, hatred of parents, abortion, putting family or school ahead of Jesus in importance, etc.) Perhaps this "big sin" may have been committed years in the past—but it is still on the person's record. To make that point, I often use this example:

If I killed someone and the police caught me and wanted to put me in jail, and then I said I wouldn't do it any more and threw my gun away (or repented, or confessed, or whatever words the sinner likes to use)—where would I go? Usually the sinner will answer "to jail anyway." Why? Because I've already killed a man and I am guilty of the murder I've already committed.

Well, you've already committed sin (name the sin he has committed) and you are already guilty of it before God. He didn't forget it. It is on your record. And even though it is in the past, you are still guilty of it now.

The point is to try to get the sinner to see himself for what he is: a guilty rebel who has broken God's law.

a. Some sinners will argue with the pastor, defend themselves, make excuses for themselves, or generally resist the law of God. They may blame others or say they were ignorant. In many ways, sinners will ". . . kick against the pricks" (Acts 9:5). In such a case, you should seek (by God's power and grace) to make your ". . . face strong against their faces" and "forehead strong against their foreheads . . ." (Ezekiel 3:8), for sinners are a ". . . rebellious house . . ." (Ezekiel 2:5–6; 3:9). In other words, continue to confront the sinner. Yet, even with good counselling, many sinners will ". . . resist the Holy Ghost . . ." (Acts 7:51). God's grace is not irresistible, and God will permit a person to reject His love in Christ if that person wills to do so.

b. Some sinners will admit their sin, but turn to self-pity. A person may begin to cry and only be sorry for himself. He may try to blame God: "There's nothing I can do," or "I've been given up." Do not agree with the sinner or comfort him in his self-pity. If the sinner appears to be sad, ask him *why* he feels that way. Self pity must be distinguished from conviction of sin.

If the person is sorry for *himself* rather than guilty for sins, he is not yet ready to trust Christ.

2. The pastor must get the sinner to see that he deserves punishment. ". . . The wages of sin is death . . ." (Romans 6:23).
"The wicked shall be turned into hell . . ." (Psalm 9:17).

God is angry with the sinner's sin. While God does not
hate any sinner as a person, but rather loves him, God is **consistent** and thus must reasonably punish the bad. In other
words, God must punish sin, or He wouldn't be consistent
with His own nature. He is therefore obligated to punish the
sinner in Hell.

a. Many unawakened sinners need to be confronted with the
fact that they have sinned and are (deservedly) on the road
to Hell; in fact, they are condemned already (John 3:18).
Many need to read Dr. John R. Rice's booklet called "Hell:
What the Bible Says About It." Many jokers and triflers
need to be confronted with sin and Hell until they stop jok-
ing and laughing. Another good booklet, published by Sword
of the Lord, is Jonathan Edwards' sermon "Sinners in the
Hands of an Angry God."

b. Some will cry or otherwise appear sad, but will in fact be
sorry for themselves, because they don't want to go to Hell
(and that's all they want), or because they are not saved
(and can't get back to the business of their life), or simply
as a human emotion without any real reason behind it. Many
sinners blame God, the church, the pastor, etc., for their
state. Do not take sides with the sinner.

c. The fact that before God (the Father) a sinner must bear
his own sins, face God's wrath, and go to Hell, will help to
destroy the false hope that many sinners hold of being saved
by trusting **God**, believing in God, following God, etc. I tell
them that if they come to God they'll be judged for their
sins and God's anger (wrath) will come down upon them.
Many Catholics will speak of "Jesus" or "Christ" or "Cristo"
and in fact mean God the Father. Point the sinner **away**
from God the Father. He needs a refuge **from** God the Father and His righteous anger; he needs to hide himself in

Jesus, the "Rock of Ages, cleft for me," (1 Timothy 2:5; John 14:6; Romans 5:8–9).

   d. Tempted though he may be, the pastor must not focus exclusively on Hell. Jesus did not die to save us from Hell, but to forgive and pay for *sin*. As a *result* of having our sins paid for, we do not go to Hell. Furthermore, a mere desire to escape from Hell does not save. It is neither Hell nor Heaven that saves, but the crucified and risen Lord Jesus Christ. Thus, the pastor should not try to put Hell in the sinner's mind by itself, but only as a means to get the sinner to see that he needs Christ. This is highly important. Sin, not Hell, is the obstacle stopping them from conversion.

3. The pastor must get the sinner to see that he is in fact **lost** in the true sense of the word, without any way out of his predicament. The sinner who is lost is one who cannot find his way home and therefore needs Jesus.

    The fact is, the sinner cannot change his own nature, cannot pay for his sins, and cannot get his sins off his record before God. "They that are in the flesh cannot please God" (Romans 8:8; cf. Jeremiah 13:23).

    Sadly, however, sinners hide in false hopes. They may consider themselves saved, but "there is a way that seemeth right unto a man, but the end thereof are the ways of death" (Proverbs 14:12). False hopes come in several types. Here are three of them:

   a. *Actions*: Following Jesus, trying to be good, cleaning up one's life, "repentance" or stopping sins, going to church, loving Jesus, keeping the Ten Commandments (but have you kept them? No? So that won't work, will it?), being baptized, "trusting Jesus day by day" which means being good minute by minute, and so on. But how can these things pay for your past sins and get them off your record (Titus 3:5)?

   b. *Feelings/experiences*: Crying over sin and confessing it (Judas did that—Matthew 27:4), feeling joy/peace/the Holy

Ghost/assurance (will you feel that way tomorrow?).

c. *Mental events*: Believing Bible doctrine, **that** Jesus died and rose again for sinners (the devil believes that too, and he's not saved. What have you got that he doesn't have; what have you done that he hasn't done?); saying the sinner's prayer (you've said it many times, it didn't work); studying the Bible; learning how to be saved (How will this pay for your sins? You must still actually **be** converted); hoping/believing that you will be saved some day (you're lost now).

The above list of false hopes is not complete. Perhaps no finite list can include all the excuses which depraved, unconverted minds can invent. The important thing is that none of these false hopes can pay for a person's sins or wipe them off his record in Heaven. Only the blood of Christ can do that.

Note: The pastor must not take too much time in explaining to the sinner **why** his false hope cannot save him. This will move the emphasis from that of confrontation and a move toward conversion over to a theological tea party, to discuss what Machen called an "idle tale." The discussion will degenerate into a theological seminar on the technicalities of salvation. Often the sinner will turn quickly from one false hope into another.)

Thus, you should not try to **teach** anything to the sinner. Hold him to the false hope he gave before. The point of exposing the false hope is not to teach him true doctrine, but instead to maintain the focus and "kick out the prop" upon which the sinner leans, so as to leave him in the unhappy but real position of being a lost sinner without hope and comfort. You do not have to explain what's wrong with the false hope, but rather "kick out the prop" and "keep the pressure on."

You said that you would get to Heaven by keeping the Ten Commandments. But you haven't kept them, so that doesn't work. Why, you committed adultery. What a terrible sin. And you turned your back on your mother. No, you broke the Ten

Commandments. And those sins are on your record before God. Trying to be better now won't get those horrible sins off your record. Trying to keep the commandments now won't pay for those terrible, dreadful sins.

Look the sinner in the eye and keep the pressure on. Do not let him "off the hook." He will try to talk about something else. Keep the pressure on him until he either "gives up" or resists the Holy Spirit (trying to outlast you and use up the time is resisting the Holy Spirit).

4. *When a sinner has "given up," he is ready to trust Jesus.* The Philippian jailor said, ". . . Sirs, what must I do to be saved?" (Acts 16:30). On the day of Pentecost people were ". . . pricked in their heart" and said to the apostles, "Men and brethren, what shall we do?" (Acts 2:37).

This moment of "giving up" occurs when a sinner (seeing his sin) comes to the end of his tricks, methods, words, and false hopes, and sees himself without hope (Luke 15:17). He may actually say something like what the Philippian jailor and the Jews at Pentecost said: "But then how *can* I be saved? Or what *do* I do to be saved?" When the sinner has given up and he is not fighting any more, he is ready to be saved. Jesus was waiting with open arms all the time.

This moment is manifested in different ways with different people. Usually, however, tears do not mean the person is ready. They are often tears of self-pity or hysterical emotion. Even if the person is convicted of sin, he must move away from raw emotion and tears and turn to Jesus. Salvation is not in conviction, but in Christ; conviction is a front porch to salvation, but not salvation itself. Usually the moment comes in humble seriousness without actual tears. One person, when asked if she could or would come to Jesus asked, "Even if you're bad?" She was saved within a few minutes.

Sometimes the emphasis is on sin rather than on the lack of a false hope: a person may be stunned by his sin and have nowhere to turn.

But sometimes the emphasis is on hopelessness. People who have tried to be saved for some time through stubbornly holding to a false hope (or one after another) may finally "give up on themselves" and think (not in a self-pitying way) that they can't or won't ever get saved. They may be surprised to hear that they can come to Christ and not be cast out (John 6:37); of course, they could have been saved before if only they had come to Christ, but they refused.

How can you recognize this moment? I have tried to give some pointers, but *I must confess that I cannot recognize this time in every case.* A pastor who could recognize this state in every case would have everyone converted who he "prayed with," and would never "pray with" anyone without that person being saved. *Discerning a person's spiritual state is a gift from God and requires His help, given through prayer.*

Note: Even a moment of conviction is not an end in itself! The human heart is deceitful and desperately wicked (Jeremiah 17:9), and will invent the most subtle of excuses, such as, "I'm trying to reach a moment of conviction," "I'm not humble yet," "I am broken now," "I can't seem to get my heart broken," "I can't seem to get rid of my false hopes," "This time I *did* get rid of my false hopes (what a wonderful thing I did)," and so on.

All these reveal an *unawakened* soul who is still trying to be saved by religious machinations, and still trying to save himself. It is one thing to use the means of grace and ask God for conviction of sin; it is another thing to attempt to "steer your own ship" and pilot yourself into salvation so that the glory and boasting belongs not to God, but to self.

The pastor should not lose sight of the fact that Christ, Himself, is the end and goal of all preaching and personal work. He, not the worker or the process, is the Savior. Sometimes it is wise to put all analysis on the shelf and simply call the sinner to come to Christ.

D. The converted sinner

When a person is ready to come to Christ, the actual act of trusting Him is quite simple. After all, Jesus called little children to come unto Him. The act of trusting Jesus may seem like an anti-climax after all the mighty struggles, but we should remember that God's ways are not our ways (Isaiah 55:8). Elijah witnessed a great wind, an earthquake, and a fire, but the Lord was not in those things (1 Kings 19:11–12). The Lord instead was present in a still, small voice (1 Kings 19:12–13).

There are two things which I show the sinner:

1. The objective side—What must the sinner *believe?*

Jesus suffered and died in your place so that you can be forgiven. God's anger against your sins was poured out upon Jesus, on the cross. If you trust Jesus, His blood washes away (pays for, covers) your sins. "For when we were yet without strength, in due time Christ died for the ungodly" (Romans 5:6). "He [Jesus] was wounded for our transgressions, he was bruised for our iniquities" (Isaiah 53:5). ". . . Being now justified [with our sins covered, taken off our record] by his blood, we shall be saved from wrath [punishment] through him (Romans 5:9).

The sinner must also believe that Jesus is alive, resurrected from the dead, at the right hand of God in Heaven. "He was received up into heaven, and sat on the right hand of God" (Mark 16:19). ". . . It is Christ that died, yea rather, that is risen again, who is even at the right hand of God, who also maketh intercession for us" (Romans 8:34). "Seek those things which are above, where Christ sitteth on the right hand of God. Set your affection on things above, not on things on the earth" (Colossians 3:1–2).

Even though a person may have heard this before, it never hurts to go through the Gospel again.

2. The subjective side—What must the sinner *do?*

". . . Believe [trust] on the Lord Jesus Christ, and thou shalt be saved . . ." (Acts 16:31). "Come unto me [Jesus said],

. . . all ye that labour and are heavy laden, and I will give you rest" (Matthew 11:28).

The sinner must personally trust, take, receive Christ. The sinner who does this receives the objective benefits which He died to give.

After going through this, I lead the sinner in a simple "sinner's prayer." Of course, the words of the prayer are just a guide, and just saying the words will not save in itself (sometimes I tell the sinner that). But if the sinner is ready to trust Christ, the prayer can be a helpful guide.

On a general level, the prayer should be directed to Jesus, not God (1 Timothy 2:5), and should include the elements of forgiveness of sin through Jesus' blood, an act of personal trust, and the element of Jesus as a real person, resurrected from the dead, and seated at God's right hand in Heaven. Here is the prayer I use:

> Jesus, I come to you. Wash my sin with your blood. I come to you, Jesus. Wash my sin with your blood. I trust you, Jesus. Wash all of my sins away with your blood. I trust you, Jesus.

This is a simple prayer that keeps the entire focus on Jesus and His Blood. We *never* say, "I trust you *to* wash all my sins away." This easily leads to doctrinal belief rather than trusting Jesus Himself.

Trusting Christ is a special act in itself. Nothing a person does throughout his life is quite the same. It can only be done once, and only needs to be done once. But it must reflect the true inner reality of resting in and trusting in Jesus alone for salvation. The marvelous encounter, the instantaneous act of trusting Christ for salvation, has many things connected with it. For instance, when a person trusts Christ, his sins are forgiven, he receives a new nature, Christ's righteousness is imputed to him (reckoned to his account), he is adopted into God's family, and so on.

Even the act itself has an active component, in that a person can choose to do it or not to do it (so it *is* something you do), although it is not a mere human work such as praying, fasting, giving up sins, dedicating oneself (so it *isn't* something you "do"), but yet the act is also passive, in that Jesus has already done all that is necessary to save and all that the sinner must do is rest in Him ("It is finished"—John 19:30), and this is a "non-act" or a "non-work," a ceasing from labor and finding a simple rest in Jesus without "doing" anything other than trusting Him (John 6:29).

However, the many-faceted nature of the human encounter with Christ is something which the *pastor* can keep in mind. It is *not* something which the *sinner* needs to keep in mind.

Trusting Christ is, for the sinner, a simple or "primitive" or "primal" act, an act "which has no parts." No one has to know *how* to do this, and the Bible never tells us *how* to trust Christ, because the Holy Spirit does this work in anyone who really wants to trust Jesus. Little children can trust Christ, and often do. The act of trusting Christ is not a noble work, not a mighty achievement of mind and will for which a person can congratulate himself. It is quite the opposite. It is receiving a free gift, a rescue, a salvation which cannot be worked out, worked up, or earned. The "how" and the details are not important. Does a person have to meditate on "how" to jump out of a burning building?

For the sinner or the pastor to turn to the details of "how" to trust Christ is to turn the focus away from Christ Himself who is "before all things" (Colossians 2:17) and to draw the mind to human works and machinery; "I'm trying to *really* rest in Him"; "Do I focus on Jesus or just open up a door in my heart? Do I walk over to Him or picture Him coming to me?" To focus on the details of "how" is to convert the sacred Gospel into the chatter of a tea party, and to excuse the Pharisee.

Nobody in the Bible who trusted Christ worried about "how" to do it, from the Philippian jailor to blind Bartimaeus to anyone else. When I trusted Jesus, I didn't think about "how." I was busy doing it. It was only a matter of seconds. Trust Jesus now and you will have all of time and eternity to meditate on the details and the consequences; to sing in Heaven and to worship the Lamb.

No, it's better to stick to the simple, old-fashioned religion. Get the sinner lost and then get him saved.

The Application

A. Ask the following questions:

1. If you died tomorrow (*after* you came and prayed today), would you go to Heaven or Hell?

   a. If the person says, "I don't know," ask, "What do you think a person should do to get to Heaven?" If the answer is correct, see if the person has done that. But generally if a person says "Hell," or "I don't know," the person is lost.

   b. If the person says "Heaven," move to question 2.

2. If you died and came before God and God said, "Why should I let you into Heaven?" what would you say to God?

   a. If the person says, "Because I'm a good person" or some other false hope, he is lost.

   b. If the person says, "Because you died for me" (talking to God, remember!) or "Because I trusted you" (to God) or even "Because I trusted Him" or "Because He died for me" (meaning God), the person is lost, having confused Jesus and God the Father. Many Catholics will make this mistake.

   c. If the person says, "Because Jesus died for me," or "Because Jesus covered my sins with His blood," or some other correct answer, go to question 3. But be sure the person has given the name of "Jesus" and not "God" or "Him."

3. How would that get you into Heaven? The idea is to see if the person understands that Jesus' blood pays for and covers sin.

Another way to say this is in question 4.

4. What has Jesus done for you—that would get you into Heaven? See if the person understands something of the atonement.

5. What did *you* do to get Jesus to cover (wash, forgive) your sins? If the person says "come to Jesus" or "trust Jesus", you can move to question 6. If the person gives a false hope, he is lost.

6. When did you do that? It should be "just now," or whatever time you think the person might have been saved. If the person gives some other time, he is usually lost.

7. Have you ever done that before? (Or, have you ever come to or trusted Jesus before in the same way?) If the person says "yes," find out what he did before. But remember that you can't be truly saved twice, so he probably has just repeated a false hope from the past.

8. How was this different from any time you did this in the past? Try to find out if there is any difference at all. Or is this just a bunch of words he has memorized and repeated?

9. What does "that" mean to you? What do you mean by that? Here the "that" is "come to Jesus" or "trust Jesus" or whatever the person has done to be saved (or has memorized!). Try to get the person to say it in his own words, not just to repeat memorized "church words."

Another way you could ask is, "How would you tell me (or another person) to come to Jesus (or trust Jesus)?"

Still another way is, "Just how did you do that?" Focus on the time of salvation. If the person starts to talk about his whole life story or the story of the whole long day, bring him back to the time when he prayed to come to Jesus. If he cannot say anything at all about that particular time, he is lost. He should be able to say at least a few words about the most important event of his life.

Very often when the person gets into his own words, a false hope will come out, like "I believe/trust *that* Jesus died for me (or can save me, or has saved me, etc.)", or "I have *asked*

Jesus to save me (without actually coming *to* Jesus)" or "It means loving Jesus (or following Jesus, or serving Jesus)," or "It means turn from all your sins," or some other false hope.

You can test whether the person has mixed coming to Jesus with something else. If he says, "I asked Jesus to forgive me," or "I prayed to Jesus to forgive me," say, "Does everyone who asks Jesus (or prays to Jesus) to be saved, get saved?" And then, "Could a person be saved without asking Jesus to save him (or praying for it)?" Many Catholics ask Jesus to save them in the Mass, "Christ have mercy," without being saved. And yet Dr. Hymers and many others have been saved without asking anything or praying a sinner's prayer by simply looking to Christ (Isaiah 45:22). A person should know that asking and praying are not the exact same thing as coming to Jesus. Coming to Jesus is just what it says—*coming to Jesus is coming to Jesus.* It is something in a class by itself, it is a special thing. It may include asking, but it is *more* than just the human act of asking. It is coming to Jesus, Himself and believing on Him.

10. If the person has answered correctly up to now, continue with: "If you had a bad thought a year from now and then died without confessing it, would you be saved?" (You may use some small sin in place of a bad thought, such as not saying grace once before you eat.) If the person says "no," he is trying to save himself by the work of being perfect. If the person says "yes," ask him why. See if he sees that Jesus died for his future sins as well as the past.

11. Then ask, "If you stopped coming to church, moved in with a prostitute, and had sex with her every night for two years, and got drunk at a bar every night for two years, and then died, *would you be a Christian or not?*" You will be surprised at how many will say, "yes," because they have in those few minutes of counselling turned the grace of God into lasciviousness. (The idea is to give a couple of gross sins over a long period of time, which a Christian will not do.) Sadly, many think they

can commit gross sins again and again without any doubt as to their salvation, although the Bible says that people who practice such sins will not go to Heaven and are not saved (1 Corinthians 6:9–11; Galatians 5:19–21; 1 John 3:9, and other verses).

Remember to say "a Christian," not "saved." The correct answer is "no," of course—ask him why. He may think he would lose his salvation, but this doesn't necessarily mean that he should be failed in the check. The important thing is that a Christian just doesn't do this sort of sin continually.

If the person says "yes," this is the antinomian position and the person is not saved. Very often people who have memorized the answers to the other questions, but without coming to Jesus and being born again, will fail on this one. They have doctrinally memorized that Jesus died for sins, but don't have the reality of it in their possession!

12. If the person has answered correctly so far, he may be saved. Now test his *attitude!* Ask him to come to church—not just any church or his "old" church, but the church where he got saved. If the person says anything other than a straight "yes," he is very likely lost and has only memorized the answers. But find out why he can't promise to come to church. Maybe you can solve the problem easily and he will come. Even if he really isn't saved, the reason he gives will shed light on his false hope and his thinking. In some cases, there are other ways to examine the person's general attitude, but this depends on the individual person.

13. In special cases it is good to ask a question which fits the individual case of the person, to see if a genuine union with Christ has taken place: "Can a person go to Heaven by trusting God?" ("yes" means the person trusts God, not Jesus, and is lost — John 14:6; 1 Timothy 2:5).

"What is Jesus like?" (Is Jesus a spirit? Is Jesus the same as God the Father? Is He angry? Is Jesus still on the cross now? Did He rise from the dead? etc.)

"Do you have to trust Jesus every second to be saved?" (Many have an idea of *continually* trusting Jesus, which is just a form of salvation by works; if they die in a bad moment when they aren't thinking about or "trusting" Jesus, they will go to Hell, or so they think.)

"Do you have to *totally* (or *completely*, or *one hundred percent,* or *in total sincerity*) trust Jesus to be saved?" (A "yes" answer may indicate salvation by works.)

"How do you know you're saved?" (The best answer is, "Because the Bible says so"—John 6:37, or "Because Jesus died for me and I came to Him." If a person says "I just know," it may mean he is trusting his feelings, or it may mean he is really born again, depending on the individual case.)

"Why weren't you saved before?" "What did you do instead of trust Jesus?" (Try to see if he understands his false hope or error of the past, or at least understands his sin and neglect of God.)

Also, you may test the person's attitude about sin and right versus wrong. You can mention particular sins the person actually committed and see if he has had a change of mind (repentance) about them. Also, if the person remains in rebellion and says something like, "I'm saved, you can't tell me I'm not, I'm not coming back, etc." this reveals that he has just memorized the answers without being saved (1 Corinthians 2:14).

14. Finally, there is the *test of time.* You can't give that test right there in the inquiry room. But tell the person who is hopefully saved that if he turns out not to be a Christian (leaves the church, or goes back to gross continual sin), he fails the test of time and reveals that he was never saved, even if he has memorized the answers to your questions (Luke 8:11–14; 1 John 2:19).

B. The course of a sample session: (We have the people read a sheet titled, "Your Biggest Problem—Sin," before we speak to them).

1. Hello, my name is Dr. Cagan, what is your name? (the person replies).
2. What kind of church or religion did you go to in the past before you came here with us? It is important to do this because it will give you insight into what the person very likely believes.
3. Note: some sinners, usually early in the talking, but sometimes later, will blurt out an important statement, usually something which the Holy Spirit has been showing them. One person said without being asked, "Do you think there has to be a definite day when a person trusts Jesus?" God had been bothering her about that very subject.
4. Why did you come forward today? What do you want Jesus to do for you? Many people, although they came forward, did not do so in order to have their sins forgiven. Some have said that they want Jesus to heal them, to give them a job, to help them with a personal problem, or something other than salvation. Pray for that problem, but then explain to the person that even if the problem were solved, he would still go to Hell for his sins at death, so there is a deeper problem to deal with, his salvation.

     If the person says, "to save me," or "to wash away my sins," continue to question 5.
5. If you died right now, where do you think you would go? Does the person consider himself saved at present, or not?
6. If you died and came before God at the gate of Heaven and God asked you, "Why should I let you into Heaven?" what would you say to God? This will give you insight into what the person's hope of salvation is. It may often be works, doctrinal belief, or some other error.
7. How would that get you into Heaven? How does this hope of yours work?
8. (If the person thinks he is saved) When did you get saved? Tell me about that time (not the whole life story, but what happened right then, the immediate context in time). What

did you *do* that got you saved, got your sins forgiven?

9. Your problem is that your sins are written in God's books. (We use a sheet with a person standing in front of God and the books open).

10. Even if you try to be good, or really become good, or go to church, or believe that Jesus exists (whatever the false hope is), that would not remove your sins from the books.

11. Only Jesus' vlood can cover your sins and wash them out of the books.

12. Where do you think Jesus *is* right now? The correct answer: in Heaven, at the right hand of God the Father. Many people think that Jesus is in the air, or already in their heart, or somewhere else. Remember that Jesus is not in the heart of any unbeliever (see Jeremiah 17:9) and that Satan is the prince of the power of the air. He is in the air around us, not Jesus, who is at the right hand of the Father in the heavenly place.

13. Is Jesus angry with you for your sins? Many people think He is, and then are afraid, or consider themselves unworthy, to come to Him. It is true that God is angry with sins, but Jesus died for sinners and will receive any sinner who comes to Him. (Note: for this reason, especially for those with Catholic ideas, you must emphasize that the person must come to Jesus, not to God.)

14. Sometimes (if the person has prayed before and feels no hope, or is looking for a particular set of thoughts or feelings to authenticate his salvation), I use John 6:37: "Him that cometh to me I will in no wise cast out." Anyone that comes to Jesus, regardless of thoughts, feelings, sins, or anything else, will be received and forgiven by Jesus.

15. If you come to Jesus and trust Him today, His Blood will cover your sins. And God won't see your sins, won't judge you for them.

16. Will you do that now? If the person seems to be awakened, pray with him. Sometimes I say, "The prayer itself is just a guide. The important thing is to come to Jesus during this

time." Sometimes I say, "Remember, come to Jesus, not to God." (Coming to God and not Jesus will get the person burned in fire!) This shows the absolute importance of Jesus' mediatorial work (John 14:6). I also tell them that Jesus is alive, seated at the right hand of God in Heaven (Mark 16:19; Colossians 3:1; 1 Peter 3:22). People need to know where Jesus is or they cannot come to Him in any real sense.

17. Then I give the person a chance to rest in another room and check the person in a few minutes. (Or sometimes I check the person immediately.) If the person has made an error, correct it, and pray with the person again, unless he or she is unawakened. (Those who make the same error again and again are almost always unconcerned, not paying attention.) I usually give them something to read, such as Edwards' "Sinners in the Hands of an Angry God," or John R. Rice's "Crossing the Deadline." Then I send them home to read it and ask them to come and see me again after hearing the next sermon in church.

With these methods, I hope and pray that many more people will be truly converted and go on to live productive Christian lives. Love the people enough to spend time with them and help them find salvation through Jesus. This is our highest calling as winners of lost souls. It is this kind of love that may well pave the way for God to send true revival to our churches one more time.

Footnotes

1. C. H. Spurgeon, "Conversion As Our Aim," from *Lectures To My Students* (New York: Robert Carter & Bros., 1889), quoted in *Encounter With Spurgeon* by Helmut Thielicke (Grand Rapids: Baker Book House, 1975), pp. 60–61.
2. F. L. Chapell, *The Great Awakening of 1740* (Philadelphia: American Baptist Publication Society, 1903), p. 133.
3. Richard Baxter, *The Reformed Pastor* (Edinburgh: Banner of Truth Trust, 1989, reprinted from the 1656 edition), pp. 94–97.
4. J. Gresham Machen, *Christianity and Liberalism* (Grand Rapids: Eerdmans, 1923, reprinted 1983), p. 66.
5. Brian H. Edwards, *Revival! A People Saturated With God* (Durham, En-

gland: Evangelical Press, 1991), p. 108.

6. Brian H. Edwards, p. 254.

7. Brian H. Edwards, p. 275.

8. Asahel Nettleton, *Sermons from the Second Great Awakening,* (Ames, IA: International Outreach, 1995 reprint), pp. 166–67.

9. John R. Rice, *Why Preach Against Sin?* (Murfreesboro, TN: Sword of the Lord, 1946), pp. 17–20.

10. C. H. Spurgeon, *Lectures To My Students,* pp. 60–61.

11. Richard Baxter, *The Reformed Pastor* (Edinburgh: Banner of Truth Trust, 1989, reprinted from the 1656 edition), pp. 94–97.

12. C. H. Spurgeon, "The Warrant of Faith," *Metropolitan Tabernacle Pulpit,* volume 9 (Pasadena, TX: Pilgrim Publications, 1979), p. 530.

13. A. T. Pierson, *The Bible and Spiritual Life* (New York: Gospel Publishing House, 1908), p. 238; quoted in Henry C. Thiessen, *Lectures in Systematic Theology* (Grand Rapids: Eerdmans, 1949), p. 359.

14. C. H. Spurgeon, "The Warrant of Faith," p. 530.

15. J. Gresham Machen, *Christianity and Liberalism,* p. 66.

16. C. H. Spurgeon, *Around the Wicket Gate* (Pasadena, TX: Pilgrim Publications), p. 57.

Epilogue
Can We Have Revival Now?

In chapter one we gave several signs that the end is near. Two of these signs are connected with apostasy in the churches:

- The rise of apostasy in Christianity (2 Thessalonians 2:3; Matthew 24:12).
- The repetition of circumstances in the days of Noah (Matthew 24:37–39).

These signs present a dark picture, which seems to be reflected in the world around us at this hour. We quoted Dr. Woodrow Kroll, who said:

> In 1900 there were 27 churches churches for every 10,000 Americans. In 1985 this figure had declined so drastically that it is painful to report. There are now less than 12 churches for every 10,000 Americans; less than half the former amount. . . . Between 3,500 and 4,000 churches close their doors each year in America. . . . By the year 2000 there will be only 33 percent of the American population who belong to a church.[1]

We quoted a survey from the *Baptist Bible Tribune* which shows that eighty-four percent of those who claim to be "born again" believe false doctrine on central Christian teachings.[2] We also quoted Billy Graham, who said: "We are a society poised on the brink of self-destruction. Our culture is plagued with crime and violence, drug abuse, racial and ethnic tension, broken families and corruption."[3]

We showed that the apostasy of our day has its roots in the false doctrines and methods of Charles G. Finney which has led to a largely unconverted church membership in our day. As Dr. Martyn Lloyd-Jones put it:

> I have no hesitation in asserting that the main cause of the state of the Christian church today, and the whole state of the world, in consequence, is the terrible apostasy that has characterized the church for the last hundred years.[4]

In view of the present darkness, many have wondered if revival is possible. Can we have another revival amid such severely apostate conditions? Many good men have said, "No! The age will go out in blackness, with no hope of revival."

In our view, that position is not correct, however. Yes, the age will indeed go out in deep apostasy, but it is clear in the book of Revelation that powerful revivals will occur, even under the terribly repressive reign of the Antichrist himself—at the *very* end of this dispensation!

Here are three reasons we believe that end-time revival is a distinct possibility in our time:

1. The Promise of Christ

First, Jesus said, "Lo, I am with you always, even unto the end of the world" (Matthew 28:20). Christ promised to be with His true followers right to the end of the age. Dr. John R. Rice said:

> The God whom some people worship is old and tired. The present-day civilization is too much for Him! Maybe He could one time give great revivals, but He cannot any more. Mankind has simply gotten to be worse than that old-fashioned God can handle—the God of some people's faith. . . . Christians with belief in that kind

of a defeated God can have no great revivals. . . . So many Christians look for the rapture as a last resort of a God who cannot cope with the present world, in a Christianity which is more or less out of date, very nice for the few who have it, but inadequate to reach multitudes. . . . Can you see the wickedness, the near-blasphemy of that kind of attitude toward God and the gospel? How God must be grieved by our defeated unbelief about revivals![5]

The promise of Christ, that He would be with us to the very end of this dispensation, makes revival a distinct possibility today, even in the midst of great apostasy.

2. The Midnight Cry

Second, we have the prophetic midnight cry, which Jesus gave in the Olivet Discourse: ". . . At midnight there was a cry made, Behold, the bridegroom cometh; go ye out to meet him. Then all those virgins arose, and trimmed their lamps" (Matthew 25:6–7).

Five of the virgins were wise, and five of them were foolish. The foolish ones were unprepared for Christ's return. ". . . And they that were ready went in with him to the marriage: and the door was shut" (Matthew 25:10). Some good men have felt that this passage refers to Jewish people at the end of the Tribulation. However, in Matthew 25:1–13 we are not told that these are Jewish people. Also, the Tribulation is not mentioned anywhere in these verses.

We hold the view that this passage indicates that a great revival will occur just before the return of Jesus for His own, in the Rapture. ". . . And they that were ready went in with him to the marriage . . ." (Matthew 25:10). We do not wish to be dogmatic, but this passage does seem to indicate that revival will come before the Rapture. Read Matthew 25:1–13 again, with that thought in mind.

3. The Revivals of the Tribulation

Third, the Bible predicts great revivals in the Tribulation period itself, immediately prior to the end of this age. Revelation 7:3–8 reveals a future ingathering of Jewish people during this brief period—a revival among the Jews—just before the end. Then, in Revelation 7:9–14, we are told of a coming mighty revival among the Gentiles of this final period. The Scripture says: ". . . These are they which came out of great tribulation, and have washed their robes, and made them white in the blood of the Lamb" (Revelation 7:14).

These prophecies seem to indicate that it is possible for real revival to appear again in the closing days of this dispensation. An *exact* replication of the days of Noah is not necessary for Jesus' prediction to be true in our time. As with any type and antitype, there may be details that don't coincide perfectly. While it is true that there was no revival in Noah's day, the prophecies we have just quoted seem to indicate that a revival can happen in our day. But we must first repudiate the false doctrines and methods of Finney and his modern followers, the methods of decisionism. We must once again preach strong sermons that include naming sin and lifting high the Gospel of Christ. Also, pastors must return to the old way of personally counselling inquirers. And we must also return to old-fashioned praying. We must cry out to God—pleading with Him to send revival.

Oh that thou wouldest rend the heavens, that thou wouldest come down, that the mountains might flow down at thy presence, As when the melting fire burneth, the fire causeth the waters to boil, to make thy name known to thine adversaries, that the nations may tremble at thy presence! When thou didst terrible things which we looked not for, thou camest down, the mountains flowed down at thy presence.

—Isaiah 64:1–3

Footnotes

1. Woodrow Kroll, *The Vanishing Ministry* (Grand Rapids, MI: Kregel Publications, 1991), pp. 31–33.
2. *Baptist Bible Tribune,* April 15, 1996, p. 28.
3. *Los Angeles Times,* May 3, 1996, p. A-10.

4. D. Martyn Lloyd-Jones, *Revival* (Wheaton, IL: Crossway Books, 1987), p. 57.
5. John R. Rice, *We Can Have Revival Now!* (Murfreesboro, TN: Sword of the Lord, 1950), pp. 116–17.

Appendices

The dark days that preceded the Great Awakening will come again unless somebody stands firmly and clearly and decidedly by the doctrine of a converted church-membership.

—F. L. Chapell, Baptist pastor, in his 1903
edition of *The Great Awakening of 1740*

Remember the days of old, consider the years of many generations.

— Dcuteronomy 32:7

Ask for the old paths, where is the good way, and walk therein, and ye shall find rest for your souls.

—Jeremiah 6:16

Fifteen Books That Will
Help a Counsellor

Here are fifteen books here which will greatly help a pastor or other counsellor.* Anyone who is interested in the subjects we have addressed in this book can procure them from a bookstore which deals with out-of-print titles.**

1. Joseph Alleine, *An Alarm to the Unconverted* (sometimes titled, *A Sure Guide to Heaven*). Published under the second title by Banner of Truth Trust, 1959. Here is the table of contents:
   1. Mistakes about conversion.
   2. The nature of conversion.
   3. The necessity of conversion.
   4. The marks of conversion.
   5. The miseries of the unconverted.
   6. Directions to the unconverted.
   7. The motives to conversion.
   First published in 1671, *An Alarm to the Unconverted* has been used by God an as instrument in revivals; it has been the means of bringing countless numbers to Christ; and it moulded the

---

* Although we do not endorse everything in these books, we believe that they will be very helpful in guiding one's thoughts out of the decisionism of our time.

** Dr. David O. Beale has a worldwide booksearching ministry. He will be able to obtain these books for you. Phone him at (864) 233-0501.

thought of the great evangelist George Whitefield. Many of the chapters can easily be converted into evangelistic sermons, particularly chapters one, four, and five. These chapters contain the type of application of the Law that awakens sinners, but is so largely absent from today's preaching.

2. Richard Baxter, *The Reformed Pastor*. First published in 1656, and reprinted by Banner of Truth Trust in 1989. Philip Doddridge said that it "should be read by every young minister before he takes a people under his care; and, I think, the practical part of it reviewed every three or four years." We would be in full agreement. This is arguably the most important book on pastoring that has ever been written.

3. Richard Baxter, *A Treatise on Conversion*. First published in 1657, and reprinted countless times. A person who sees the folly of decisionism in our day should study this book carefully. It will be a guide out of decisionist darkness. Here are the chapter titles:
   1. Nature of conversion—change of mind.
   2. Nature of conversion—change of heart.
   3. Nature of conversion—change of affections.
   4. Nature of conversion—change of life.
   5. Necessity of conversion.
   6. Self-application—"Am I converted?"
   7. Miseries of the unconverted.
   8. Benefits of conversion.
   9. Appeal to the unconverted.
   10. Hindrances, with corresponding directions.
   11. Hindrances and directions—continued.

4. Brian H. Edwards, *Revival! A People Saturated with God* (Durham, England: Evangelical Press, 1991). It will set the heart longing for real revival. Multiple examples from history are given.

5. John H. Gerstner, *Jonathan Edwards, Evangelist* (Morgan, PA: Soli Deo Gloria Publications, 1995 reprint). Dr. Gerstner presents Edwards' teachings in a crisp, modern style. It also sys-

tematizes the thinking of this great preacher, and portrays him as an evangelist, concerned with revival and the salvation of souls. Well worth reading and re-reading.

6. Matthew Mead, *The Almost Christian* (Morgan, PA: Soli Deo Gloria Publications, 1989). Though we would not recommend John MacArthur, who wrote the introduction, because of his view on incarnational Sonship and other matters, we strongly recommend the book itself. It contains a series of sermons given by Mead on self-examination (2 Corinthians 13:5). These are the kind of sermons that need to be preached in our pulpits today.

7. Iain H. Murray, *Revival and Revivalism* (Edinburgh: Banner of Truth Trust, 1994). Read chapter fourteen first, then the whole book. Our little book on decisionism, which you have just read, is an outgrowth of the historical insights given here by Murray.

8. Iain H. Murray, *Spurgeon vs. Hyper-Calvinism* (Edinburgh: Banner of Truth Trust, 1995). A good introduction to Spurgeon as an evangelist; corrects overemphasis on various doctrines.

9. Asahel Nettleton, *Sermons from the Great Awakening* (Ames, IA: International Outreach, 1995). The only book we know of that gives fifty-three of Nettleton's sermons, most of them complete, plus seventeen remarks on scriptural passages, and twelve miscellaneous remarks on important subjects by the great evangelist. Dr. Hymers has preached over thirty of these sermons from our own pulpit. Everyone needs this book. You can order it from International Outreach, Inc., P.O. Box 1286, Ames, IA 50014, U.S.A. Phone (515) 233-2932.

10. C. H. Spurgeon, *New Park Street Pulpit* and *Metropolitan Tabernacle Pulpit*. Sixty-two volumes, published by Pilgrim Publications, P.O. Box 66, Pasadena, TX 77501, U.S.A. No other sermon set is as valuable. All preachers should have it.

11. Index to the *New Park Street Pulpit* and *Metropolitan Tabernacle Pulpit*. This index is a must. It gives every Spurgeon sermon, both by title and by text. All who buy the Spurgeon

sermons should have it. Available from Pilgrim Publications.

12. Solomon Stoddard, *A Guide to Christ* (Ligonier, PA: Soli Deo Gloria Publications, 1993). Reprinted from the 1816 Northampton edition. Though we would disagree with Stoddard's "Half-Way Covenant," which admitted unconverted members to the Lord's Supper as a means of converting grace, we recommend this book, particularly the section titled, "Directions How to Guide Souls Through the Work of Conversion." Well worth reading and meditating on; it is a must for every library.

13. Joseph Bellamy, *Sin, the Law, and the Glory of the Gospel* (International Outreach, P. O. Box 1286, Ames, IA 50014. Phone (515) 233-2932). Joseph Bellamy, one of the key figures in the Great Awakening, shows how conviction of sin by the Law is critical to a real conversion.

14. Anthony Burgess, *Spiritual Refining—The Anatomy of True and False Conversion* (volumes 1 and 2). Two books on the use of self-examination. They show how true conversion can be distinguished from its counterfeit. (Order from International Outreach, P. O. Box 1286, Ames, IA 50014. Phone (515) 233-2932.)

15. *Village Hymns for Social Worship,* edited by Asahel Nettleton. six hundred hymns, one hundred eighty of them set to music. Over fifty by John Newton, forty-eight by Isaac Watts, along with hymns by William Cowper, Phillip Doddridge, Timothy Dwight, and others. Most of these great hymns have been lost to this generation as a result of Finney's decisionism, the resulting change in evangelistic preaching, and the adoption of hymns that fit the decisionist message. The discontinuing of these older hymns, which present true biblical conversion, has resulted in them being replaced by modern Gospel songs and choruses in most hymnals. *This is a hymn book every pastor in America needs to have, with hymns that need to be reintroduced to our churches* (International Outreach, P. O. Box 1286, Ames, IA 50014. Phone (515) 233-2932).

Appendix 2

Conversion Testimonies

The following are six testimonies which were given at our church in Los Angeles. They represent "hopeful" conversions, since they have not yet passed the test of time (Luke 8:13). This test requires many years. We present them here as examples of the kind of testimonies that come through using the methods given in this book.

Testimony 1
The hopeful conversion of a thirteen-year-old boy
It was about seven o'clock on a Saturday night, November 30, 1996. Dr. Bob Jones, Jr. was preaching on sin and judgment. As he was preaching, I was getting more and more aware of my sins recorded in God's books, and the judgment that awaited me if I did not have them erased. As he continued preaching, I was still thinking of my sins. I knew they had not yet been blotted out by Jesus' blood. Then I thought of many foolish times that I had tried to trick my way and learn my way into conversion, but never before had I looked upon my sins as I did then.

It was not so much Hell that I feared, but it was that fact of not having my sins washed out of God's books in Heaven, by Jesus' blood. I knew that Jesus will wash away anyone's sins who will come to Him. Realizing that I had let the golden opportunity to be saved slip away many times before, I felt I would take the next opportunity that I had, rather than let my heart become more hardened and leave behind yet another opportunity, which had become such a habit to me.

As I listened to Dr. Jones with a deep conviction of my sins I remembered 2 Timothy 3:15, "And that from a child thou hast known the holy scriptures, which are able to make thee wise unto salvation through faith which is in Christ Jesus." Now, if there was another verse better for me I would like to have seen it. It certainly applied to my case. I had known the Scriptures, and had been in church every Sunday, and had knowledge of my state of going to Hell, but did not do anything about it. Part of the reason was that I kept trying to learn my way into Heaven. Knowing the plan of salvation, I was always trying to fool and trick the counsellors by trying to give them the right answers, learning, and learning. Every time a sermon was preached I was trying to learn how to be saved. Every time I went to the pastor's office, I tried to find the right answer to every question, trying to "pass" and become a member of the church. What a fool I was to do this. I was ever learning and never able to come to a knowledge of the truth. I should have been thinking more about passing from death unto life.

I began to see how dreadful my sins were in the sight of an almighty and sovereign God, who could throw me into Hell at any moment for my wickedness and disobedience against Him. It was not what I could do to be converted, but what Jesus had already done for me. I, as many other people do, was trying to come to Jesus my own way, with a rebellious heart and mind, that kept trying my own way, as well as trying to "fake" my way, not into Heaven, but into the church. In this case I was not even concerned about Heaven or Hell, not even fearing God. My state was indeed a horrible one that was driving me farther from salvation in Jesus.

Dr. Jones was finishing up the sermon. I was ready to get this matter settled once and for all.

When the invitation was given I went to the pastor's study, not thinking about learning, but having my heart and mind focused on my salvation through Jesus' blood. Then, for the first time, I simply fell on Jesus, that is (in my own words) the best possible way I can describe it. The falling was like me jumping off a tall building and falling on a giant pillow. Jesus is the pillow. Note, it was not the prayer that saved my soul from Hell, but the simple belief or falling on Jesus that saved me. Oh, what a glorious thing it is to know that your sins are washed away by the blood of Jesus!

Now I'm telling you that all salvation is by the grace of God. God gave me an awakening to see my sins before His eyes and to see the condition of my trickery and deceitfulness against Him that would have driven me to Hell and damnation had it not been for His grace. There has never been and never will be a person that got converted by trying to work their way, or talk their way, into Heaven. The blood of Jesus can wash away the sins of as many people as will come to Him. I am most grateful for God sending His Son Jesus to wash away my sins. I know I will never be able to do anything to repay Him in any way, except to do everything the Bible says to the best of my ability.

Testimony 2
The hopeful conversion of a middle-aged woman, long halting between religion and salvation
God drew me into this church and out of decisionism. When I came into this church, I thought I was a Christian already because of what I knew and had learned. But I came to realize that I wasn't converted.

At first I didn't believe the pastor because of an earlier religious experience that had strongly deluded me. Also, I knew that I wasn't as bad as I could be. But the more I listened to the sermons, the more I saw he wasn't just preaching to the lost who were visiting the church. He was preaching to me.

Last September I went to the pastor's study, after the invitation, to tell the pastor I was afraid that I wasn't saved. The first time I had been received into the membership of the church, I had been resting on an experience that I now know to be false. I had been deceived. I continued to halt between two opinions, finding it hard to understand how I could be so wrong.

Sunday, September 22, 1996, I went to see the pastor as I'd

done countless times before. But this time I was trembling, fearful I'd already been given up, fearful it was too late, fearful I'd never get saved. The pastor spoke to me kindly and reminded me of my need for Jesus. As I knelt to pray, I looked to Him by faith.

In that moment I didn't have any particular feeling. I'd had that before and it didn't save me. I didn't have any particular experience. I'd had that before and it didn't save me. Nothing I knew or believed or had experienced could save me: simply and only Jesus.

I'd seen myself as a sinner for years. I'd seen myself as hopeless at different times. I'd seen myself as deserving of Hell because of all my sin and especially for having rejected time and again the love of Christ and His offer to pay for my sins. But that simple look to Jesus was all it took. There were no flashing lights. There was no overwhelming emotion that swept over my soul.

Now my sins are covered by the precious blood of Jesus. He has drawn me out of sin and given me a life worth living. I'm thankful for this church, for her pastor, and for the other people God put in my life to help me come to Christ. Now I don't have to pretend to be a Christian any longer.

The Bible says in John 6:37, "All that the Father giveth me shall come to me; and him that cometh to me I will in no wise cast out." God the Father has given me to Jesus. By His grace and mercy I have come to Him. What a wonderful promise Jesus has made to me!

Testimony 3
The hopeful conversion of a twelve-year-old girl
On January 5, 1997, I read a little book on Hell and the last judgment. As I was reading it, the Holy Spirit convicted me of my sins. I knew I would have to face God at the last judgment and be cast into Hell. I wanted to trust Jesus through my feelings and thoughts instead of faith. Instead of worrying about my sins, I thought about the method of being saved. Every Sunday I came to the pastor's office, and every time I went out still lost and still clinging to my own beliefs. Every chance I got of being saved I refused, and re-

jected Jesus.

Jesus died on the cross and shed His blood so a sinner like me could be saved, and all I had to do was trust Jesus through faith. The Holy Spirit showed me what a horrible sinner I was and how I needed Jesus' forgiveness, now. The counsellors talked to me. I finally gave up my feelings and my thoughts on conversion. That evening I trusted Jesus. The instant I believed on Jesus, He washed all of my sins with His blood.

Jesus canceled all my sins, and gave me eternal life in Heaven. Jesus forgave my sins and saved me from Hell. I will not be judged by God for my sins because Jesus washed them all away. He took away the great burden of sin away from me. Jesus took the fear of death and Hell away.

Jesus made it so easy for me to be saved. All I had to do was trust Him, just put simple faith on Jesus. Not a lot of strong faith, because how could such a wicked sinner like me ever have strong faith. I just put simple little faith on Jesus and instantly He washed my sins away. I do not deserve Jesus' forgiveness, but instead I deserve Hell. God loved me so much He sent Jesus to die on the cross for me so that I could be saved. God had so much mercy on me as a lost sinner, even when I continually rejected Jesus every Sunday and refused to give up my feeling of assurance of salvation. The Holy Spirit was convicting me of my sins.

God showed me through the counsellors that my feelings have nothing to do with salvation and that *God had to feel that I was converted, not me*. It was Jesus who saved me from my sins, it was nothing I could do.

Testimony 4
The hopeful conversion of a Roman Catholic
At the beginning of December 1996, I was invited to come to this church. I was given a Bible tract to read. What it said interested me. What it said was different than what tracts from other churches said. Reading it, I realized that by faith in the blood of Jesus my dirty sins are forgiven.

When I came to the church to hear the sermon, for the first time I realized that Jesus is the only one who can wash my sins and only by Him could I come to God. I was very happy to know this because before knowing this I was lost. Because of my sins I didn't deserve the mercy of God and I was going straight to Hell, but the Lord Jesus loves us even though we be the worst of sinners. If we come to Him and trust in Him, He will cleanse us of our sins with His precious blood. When the invitation was given to go to the pastor's office, I went.

The third Sunday I came to the church, I thought I was saved because I prayed. Four months passed, but then I had a doubt that I was converted. Again I returned to the pastor's office and they told me I wasn't saved. I kept going forward, but I only became more confused. I couldn't find how to come to Jesus. I thought that by myself or by asking Jesus to forgive me my sins I could be saved. I was getting desperate because I couldn't find how to come to Jesus.

Finally one Sunday, in the sermon the pastor gave, I felt that everything he said was directed at me. I even thought, "How is it that the pastor knows all this about me?" That morning I didn't go to the pastor's office, though I should have. I went home when the service ended. I was thinking a lot about the words the pastor said, that you could only come to the Lord Jesus if God the Father drew you. I was thinking about this and was praying that God in His mercy would draw me to His Son, Jesus, to forgive my sins, and so it was. That evening it was different for me when I went to the pastor's office. Everything was opened for me. I didn't find obstacles or confusion. Thanks to the mercy of God, I was drawn to His Son, Jesus, and He erased my sins by His precious blood. Thanks to Jesus, now I'm saved for the glory of God.

Testimony 5
The hopeful conversion of a middle-aged black man
On the evening of December 15, 1996, at approximately 9:05 p.m., I became so convicted of sin, so hopelessly lost, that I just threw

myself at the feet of Jesus. At that moment I put my trust upon the Lord Jesus. He saved me. He washed my sins away by His blood, that I may have eternal life.

Week after week, before coming to Jesus, I would come forward at the invitation, go into the pastor's office for counsel, convinced that I would go to Heaven because I was such a good person. Yes, I was so arrogant that I truly believed that as a sinner that my being good and doing good deeds, promising to never sin again, would save me. Each time I left the pastor's office I was more depressed than the last time. I was so broken down over a period of time, all that was left for me to do was to think about my salvation.

Then one Sunday morning I heard a sermon by Dr. R. L. Hymers where he talked about a bird in a tower. He told about a bird flying and hitting a glass window over and over again, not realizing that it could never penetrate the glass. As he talked, I realized that I was that bird in the tower. I was doing the same thing over and over without getting saved. For once, I knew that I had never trusted Jesus. Jesus never knew me. I started feeling so bad about myself that my sin made it difficult for me to work or sleep. I knew now that I was rejecting God's plan for my eternal salvation.

Seeing that I was like that bird in the tower awakened me to the fact that I must come to Jesus for my salvation, for there was nothing that I could do to save myself. Jesus was my only hope.

On December 15, 1996, on my knees, with tears in my eyes, I came to Jesus to put my trust upon Him and have Him wash my sins away by His blood so that I would have eternal life.

God gave Jesus, His only begotten Son, to hang on the cross, to pay for my sins so that I could have eternal life.

Testimony 6
The hopeful conversion of an Hispanic man
This is my testimony. I came to the church about four years ago. I was learning the word of our Lord Jesus.

The first time I came I didn't know what it was about. I was trying to understand what Dr. Hymers was preaching. I didn't know anything, absolutely nothing. Nothing from before mattered to me. I was lost because I didn't know anything, absolutely nothing. My mind was darkened, but by the revelation of our Lord Jesus my mind was opened to understand His Holy Word.

I'm thankful also to Him that He has forgiven all my sins, that He washed my sins with His precious blood, so I could be saved by his blessing. He's washed my sins with His blood.

Also I'm thankful to the people who invited me to this church. Also I'm thankful to the good people here who try to bring others to Jesus so that your soul is with Jesus because when one dies it will be revealed in Heaven whether one is really saved or not when you stand before God. This is how I came to trust in Him, His faith, that He is great above all in this nation because if it weren't for Him, we who have done many bad things, like the people in the world that have done so many bad things, we would all go to Hell. But I give thanks to the Lord Jesus that He has forgiven me.

Now I do His work. I don't do it for me or other people, but that He might be glorified and for these people who have never heard the word of our Lord Jesus, as our Savior. This makes me want to continue serving Him so that His name may be glorified and other people may come and get saved in our church.

Also, I give thanks for Dr. Hymers' preaching, and for the translation of Dr. Cagan. Also I'm thankful to God that He has delivered me from many difficulties and also from many things because it is not very easy to be a Christian. One has to go through many trials in his life. I've had many problems. By His blessing I've been brought through them all. I've also seen that it's not very pleasant to be humiliated in front of others. I've been humiliated a lot by friends and family. I remember when I started coming, they were saying to me, "Why are you going to this church?" I told them it was because here the Word of our Lord Jesus is preached.

In this way I'm thankful to the Lord Jesus for giving His life for us sinners. For this reason I'm serving Him. He gives me strength and energy to continue in my work. He delivers me from many things. People try to lead me in bad paths. I say, "No thanks."

If it weren't for Him, who could I trust? I couldn't trust anyone, only Him because He is great and powerful. If I trust a friend, would he would lay down his life for me? He wouldn't give me anything. For this reason I'm very grateful to our Lord Jesus, our Savior. I ask our Lord Jesus to help us, give us strength and energy to continue ahead and that He send revival to us and bring our family, the children, to salvation.

Without Him we can do nothing. For His blessing we are close for Him to send this revival that we're praying for, so that He will draw our families little by little. Because it's very hard for our families to come because they are hardened. They don't know the truth.

I've never seen a revival. I've only listened about it on cassettes and in what Dr. Hymers has preached. I pray for God to send a revival to reach my parents. They're far from me. I'd like to see them, to talk with them about Him; my brother, my sisters too. By His blessing I pray the darkness where they are will be removed, and that they will come to trust Him when someone speaks to them.

When I accepted Jesus, I felt like a different person, because I trusted Him and He washed my sins by His precious blood shed on the cross of Calvary. I want to continue ahead serving Him that others come to this church so that Jesus may forgive them too.

Sham Conversion

by C. H. Spurgeon

They feared not the LORD . . .
They feared the LORD, and served their own gods . . .
Unto this day . . . they fear not the LORD . . .
—2 Kings 17:25, 33–34

It is as needful to warn you against the false as it is to urge you to the true. Conversion, which is a divine change, is imitated, and the spurious palmed off as genuine. This answers the devil's purpose in several ways: it eases the conscience of the double-minded, adulterates the church, injures its testimony, and dishonors true religion.

I. Their First Estate.
". . . They feared not the LORD . . ." (2 Kings 17:25).

1. They had little or no religion of any sort.
2. But they were near a God-fearing people, and near to king Hezekiah, under whom there had been a great revival. Such influence creates a great deal of religiousness.

II. Their Shame (False) Conversion.
". . . They feared the LORD . . ." (2 Kings 17:33).

1. They were wrought upon by fear only; the "lions" were their evangelists, and their teeth were cutting arguments.

2. They were instructed by an unfaithful priest; one of those who had practised calf-worship, and now failed to rebuke their love of false gods. Such persons have much to answer for.

3. But their conversion was radically defective, for:
   - There was no repentance.
   - No expiatory sacrifice was offered on God's one altar.
   - The false gods were not put away (verse 29).
   - While sin reigns grace is absent.
   - They rendered no obedience to Him. Even their worship was will-worship. "They feared the Lord, and *served* their own gods;" a very significant distinction.
   - The religious drunkard. See him weep! Hear him talk! He has a dread of God, but he serves Bacchus.
   - The saintly skinflint. He has "a saving faith" in the worst sense.

III. Their Real Estate.
"Unto this day . . . they fear not the LORD" (2 Kings 17:34).

1. They own Him not as God alone.
2. They act so as to prove that they are not His. See the future history of these Samaritans in the book of Nehemiah.

In real conversion there must be:
- Idol-breaking.
- Sin and self must be abandoned.
- Concentration.
- Our only God must be adored and served.

—Metropolitan Tabernacle Pulpit Number 2,928.

Author's Note: C. H. Spurgeon, "Sham Conversion," condensed by David Otis Fuller, in *Spurgeon's Sermon Notes*, pp. 51–52. This sermon is given in full in the *Metropolitan Tabernacle Pulpit,* Volume 51, pp. 145–56. A tape-recorded sermon based on "Sham Conversion" by Dr. Hymers is available for $5.00. Write to P. O. Box 15308, Los Angeles, CA 90015.

Appendix 4

Historical Revivals

by Rev. Gilbert Egerton*

"Pentecost": The First Great Revival of the Church

Pentecost marked the first great revival in the history of the Christian church. So powerful and efficacious was this outpouring of the Holy Spirit, that three thousand souls were born again in one day (Acts 2). This was just the beginning of a marvellous dispensation of divine grace. Great multitudes of souls were swept into the Kingdom of God during the years which followed. In a comparatively short space of time, the Christian church was established all over the ancient Roman Empire. These developments can only be explained in terms of a great and glorious revival of religion. The gracious revival following the church's first Pentecost was characterized by powerful praying, bold preaching, fierce persecution, great joy, and multiplied conversions.

During the latter half of the third century, Eusebius, the celebrated church historian, wrote:

Who could describe those vast collections of men that flocked to the religion of Christ and the illustrious concourse in the houses of worship? On whose account, not content with ancient buildings, they erected spacious churches in all the cities.[1]

---

* This appendix is an excerpt from *Flame of God* by Gilbert Egerton, Ambassador Publications, Belfast, Northern Ireland. Reproduced with the author's permission, it contains a few minor abridgements.

Harnack estimated that in A.D. 303 the Christian community in Asia Minor represented almost half of the total population.

The secret of the vigor and vitality of the New Testament church was due entirely to renewed baptisms of the Holy Ghost. There is scarcely a chapter in her history that is not adorned with the glorious blessings that accompany spiritual revival.

It is a sobering fact to observe how rapidly a living, vibrant, spiritual church can become utterly dead and "backslidden." The innate tendency of the life of the church is toward spiritual decline. Apart from a continuous work of grace or a special season of spiritual awakening, the most lively church will soon decline.

Frequently, and at critical junctures, God has interposed to revive His work when spiritual deadness has set in. During a season of special divine visitation, an extraordinary quickening of spiritual life among believers takes place and multitudes of careless sinners are won to Christ.

Modern Era of Great Revivals
The Great Protestant Revival (16th Century)

Following the early church era, and passing over the period of the Middle Ages, we come to the era of modern revivals. The Protestant revival which began in the fourteenth century under Wycliffe, and continued in the fifteenth century under Huss, developed great momentum during the sixteenth century under Luther, Zwingli, Knox, Calvin, and a host of other kindred reformers. This notable period of spiritual awakening marked a great crisis in the history of civilization as in the history of religion. The Reformation which brought to an end the prolonged Dark Ages gave birth to the modern era. The dawn of this new period in modern history emancipated the human mind and led the way to intellectual and spiritual freedom. The return to biblical Christianity led civilization out of priestcraft and spiritual darkness into vital experimental religion.

The Reformation was supremely a revival. It marked for a vast multitude the recovery of faith. It was a rebirth in the world of primitive evangelistic Christianity and lighted myriads of human hearts with the flame of spiritual joy.[2]

The Reformation was a great and general revival of religion during which tens of thousands of souls were born again. This gracious spiritual awakening profoundly affected Germany, Switzerland, France, Holland, and Great Britain; also to a considerable degree Spain and Italy. The saving truths of the Word of God became so widespread and deeply rooted in the hearts of the people, that the Church of Rome tried in vain to halt its progress by kindling the fires of persecution. Without doubt the Protestant Reformation in the sixteenth century was the greatest revival of religion that the church witnessed since the days of the apostles.

The Puritan Revival (17th Century)

The record of the Puritan revival during the seventeenth century is really the story of the English Bible. The beginning of the Puritan spiritual awakening can be traced to the sacrificial labors of Tyndale and his associates who gave the common people the Word of God in their own language. The Word of God so profoundly changed the life of the nation that Richard Baxter exclaimed, "England is likely to become a land of saints and a pattern of holiness to the world."[3]

The nation bound itself to God in holy obedience. The Bible was placed on the table of the House of Commons and recognized as the fount of its laws and the inspiration of its life. Vital godliness became the indispensable qualification for public office. Swearing, drunkenness, and impurity were criminal offences. Every theater in the land was closed. England became a refuge of the oppressed, the tower and strength of Protestantism in Europe. It never stood higher among the nations than in the days of Cromwell's protectorate.[4]

The great Puritan revival produced many notable preachers, among whom were Owen, Baxter, Goodwin, and the immortal Bunyan, whose writings have enriched the world ever since.

Over a period of ten years during the Puritan era, twenty thousand of England's best citizens crossed the Atlantic to America due to the cruel tyranny and oppression of the Stuarts. The development of the Commonwealth in the "new world" was a direct outcome of Puritan influence. From the days of the Pilgrim Fathers, America has been the home of numerous revivals which have diffused worldwide blessing.

The Moravian Revival (18th Century)

One of the greatest outpourings of the Spirit since the days of the apostles took place in 1727 among the Moravian Brethren at Herrnhut in Germany. For centuries the followers of John Huss, the great martyred Bohemian Reformer, had endured cruel persecution, fleeing from imprisonment and torture. They at last found refuge at Herrnhut in Saxony on the estate of a young Christian nobleman called Count Zinzendorf. Prior to the revival, the Brethren comprising this community were given to doctrinal disputes, heated arguments, and endless divisions. As a result of this grievous state of affairs, the more spiritual leaders became deeply concerned and began crying mightily to God for His intervention. Prayer was graciously answered, and revival broke forth. A definite unmistakable outpouring of the Holy Spirit took place on the entire congregation, which was absolutely indescribable.

We are apt to think of the glorious methods of the awakening as the greatest since Pentecost. We must trace Methodism to its source, and its source was the Moravian revival of 1727. Through the Moravians, both John and Charles Wesley came into the light. Much of their theology they got from the Moravian Brethren. Out of Methodism came the Salvation Army and scores of other movements. . . . Through Count Zinzendorf God set in motion spiritual currents that have revolutionized the world. It is doubtful if any other man has been so mightily used since the days of the apostle Paul. Had it not been for him, there might never have been a Moravian Church of unparalleled missionary fame nor a Methodist Church with its Wesleys, nor a Salvation Army with its Booths.[5]

On August 13, 1727, a remarkable revival took place among the children at Herrnhut and Bertholdorf. On August 25, the ministry of continual prayer began which continued for over a hundred years. In January1728 they held their first missionary meeting, and in 1731 the Moravian Missions began, which have been a tremendous force in the evangelisation of the heathen.

> This small Church in twenty years called into being more missions than the whole evangelical Church had done in two centuries. This great missionary fervour was the direct result of the mighty outpouring of the Holy Spirit at Herrnhut.[6]

The Eighteenth Century Revival

"The religious awakening under Wesley is one of the most important events in modern religious history."[7]

England, at the beginning of the eighteenth century, has been described as "a miniature Dark Age in the history of modern civilization."[8] Frightening degeneracy, profligacy, and corruption were prevalent everywhere and increasing. Of this period Rev. Rye said:

> These times were the darkest age that England has passed through in the last three hundred years. Anything more deplorable than the condition of the country, as to religion, morality, and high principle, is very difficult to conceive.[9]

Under the preaching of the Wesleys and Whitefield and their associates, a wonderful era of revival broke forth. As a result tens of thousands were converted, and the churches throughout England, Scotland, and Ireland were revitalized. This tidal wave of divine blessing extended to the British colonies in America where, under the ministry of Edwards, Tennents, and others, a powerful revival spread widely. So numerous were the outbreaks of revival, this period has since become known as the era of "The Great Awakening."

The Methodist revival was born in a prayer meeting. John Wesley records on January 1, 1739:

Mr. Hall, Kinchin, Ingrim, Whitefield, Hutchins and my brother Charles were present for our "Love Feast" [Communion] in Fetter Lane, with about sixty of our Brethren. About 3 a.m. as we were continuing instant in prayer, the power of God came mightily upon us, insomuch that many cried out for joy and many fell to the ground. . . . It was a Pentecostal season indeed.[10]

When Whitefield left for America, Wesley carried on the work in England. Following the example of Whitefield, after the established churches had closed to him, he began to preach in the open air with tremendous success. During Wesley's ministry it is estimated he travelled 250,000 miles and preached forty thousand sermons, sometimes to twenty thousand people at one time. As a result of Wesley's Spirit-anointed labors, a revival of religion spread all over the British Isles.

Whitefield crossed the Atlantic thirteen times and travelled extensively in the British Isles. Wherever he went, thousands gathered to hear him preach. Only eternity will fully reveal the far reaching effects of his mighty ministry.

The Great Awakening in America (1735)

The Great Awakening in America began in 1735 in Northampton under the ministry of Jonathan Edwards, and continued unabated for about twenty-five years. The leaders in this revival included the Tennents, Davenport, and Whitefield.

The preaching of the Gospel was attended with the most wonderful power in every part of New England. Revivals gave new life and multiplied numbers to the churches. It cannot be doubted that at least fifty thousand souls were added to the churches of New England out of a population of 250,000 . . . not less than one hundred fifty new Congregational churches were established in twenty years. The increase of Baptist churches was still more wonderful, rising from nine to four hundred in number, with a total membership of three hundred thousand members. There was a similar growth in the Presbyterian and other churches . . . tens of thousands bowed before the majesty of truth.[11]

From Northampton the revival spread to Suffield, Sunderland, Enfield, and Northfield, etc. From these centers it spread throughout New England and the Middle States. The powerful ministry of George Whitefield stirred the whole country. The wonderful and widespread response of the people to the Gospel was due to the fact that the Holy Spirit had so prepared their hearts that they were longing to hear it. This revival revolutionised the religious and moral character of not only individuals but the entire country.

The Second Great Awakening (1800)

During the winter of 1794, twenty-three New England ministers issued a joint circular letter calling on church people to pray for revival. The response was overwhelming and, as a result, the most far-reaching revival in American history began. It lasted well into the nineteenth century. This significant spiritual awakening began in the year 1800 as the result of a concentrated prayer effort.

Although Presbyterians started this revival, it was the Baptists and especially the Methodists who carried it on. Men like Francis Asbury and Peter Cartwright played a leading role. The Camp meetings were a special feature.

> During the main revival period, the Methodists could boast an average yearly increase of two thousand members. The Methodist Western Conference had a membership of twenty-seven hundred before the revival—after the revival, numbers leaped to twelve thousand. In Kentucky from 1799 to 1803 an estimated ten thousand were added to the Baptist churches. The Presbyterians also gained.[12]

> The nineteenth century was the Golden Age for Evangelical Christianity in America. It began with the far-reaching revival of 1800. . . . A period of drought in the 1840s was ended by the remarkable revival of 1857–58. . . . During the nineteenth century, evangelists carried "revival brands" from generation to generation. Men like Peter Cartwright and Asahel Nettleton [were prominent].[13]

American Revival (1857–1858)

One of the most remarkable revivals in the history of the Christian church was that which swept over the United States in the middle of the nineteenth century. It was born in prayer and carried forward through prayer. This great spiritual awakening has become known as the "Revival of 1858."

> The Revival of 1858 should be known as "the Revival of the United Prayer Meeting" for it was, throughout its course, the chief and almost sole instrument of the Divine Spirit. . . . It was not linked with any outstanding personality. . . . The Spirit of God awakened a great thirst for God. . . . The whole land was alive with daily prayer meetings. It was in these daily, united prayer meetings that the majority of conversions took place.[14]

Growing corruption marked the years preceding this revival. Crimes of violence rapidly increased. "Corruption was prevalent and unashamed in commercial and political life."[15] Early in 1856 God's people began to pray definitely for a mighty revival. Daily prayer meetings were held in Boston for several years, also in Fulton Street, New York. In some of these prayer meetings, as many as twelve thousand gathered daily to wait upon God. "A divine influence seemed to pervade the whole land, especially the northern states. It is estimated that during this revival not less than five hundred thousand souls were gloriously converted.

> The winter of 1857–58 will be remembered as the time when a great revival prevailed throughout all the northern states. It swept over the land with such power that for a time it was estimated not less than fifty thousand conversions occurred in a single week. This revival was carried on to a large extent through lay influence, so much as almost to throw the ministers into the shade.[16]

People seemed to prefer meetings for prayer than preaching. Answers to prayer were constant and striking. The windows of Heaven were opened and the Spirit of God was poured out like a flood. The following account was published in a newspaper at the time:

> Such a time as the present was never known since the days of the apostles for revivals. Revivals now cover our land, sweeping all before them, exciting the earnest cry from thousands, "What must I do to be saved?" Ministers, baptised with the Holy Ghost, preach with new power and earnestness. Meetings are held for prayer . . . with the most astonishing results. Large cities and towns from Maine to California are sharing in this great and glorious work.[17]

Some authorities have fixed the number of converts during this revival to approximately one million. Accounts of this great outpouring stirred the whole English-speaking world and inspired many Christians in other countries to seek a divine visitation.

1958 Revival in Ulster

The remarkable 1859 revival in Ulster originated in Connor, Co. Antrim. For years Rev. T. H. Moore, a godly Presbyterian minister, labored faithfully with little outward success. He often read accounts of revival and preached on this subject to his congregation. Reports of revival in America stirred him to promote one among his own people. The possibility of revival began to grip the hearts of some Christians and it became the subject of much earnest prayer.

In 1857 the Sunday school teachers began to hold a weekly prayer meeting. An intense desire to win souls for Christ seized the workers. About this time, four young men—McQuilken, Meneely, Wallace, and Carlisle began to meet regularly in an old schoolhouse near Kells, to pray for a mighty revival. Other likeminded brethren joined them, and soon definite conversions began to occur as a result. Prayer meetings multiplied and conversions were a daily occurrence until Ulster was manifestly ablaze with holy fire.

"In the parish of Connor there were at least one hundred prayer-meetings going on week by week. From Connor as a centre, district after district became influenced by the Revival Movement."[18]

"The revival spread in mighty power all over the North of Ireland. From first to last the revival was a record of answered prayer. Never was there such a time of secret and public prayer."[19]

> Revival is like a forest fire. In 1859 the Heavenly fire was leaping and spreading in all directions through Antrim, Down, Derry, Tyrone, and the other counties of Ulster. To this day, 1859 is remembered as the pre-eminent year of grace.[20]

It is estimated that approximately one hundred thousand souls were saved in Ulster as a result of the 1859 Awakening.

The 1959–60 Revival in England and Scotland

In 1859, the heavenly rain cloud, that so graciously refreshed the American Church in the previous year, crossed the Atlantic, outpoured upon Ulster an unspeakable blessing, and then hovered over the whole extent of the British Isles.[21]

Around the year 1859 England and Scotland were blessed with the ministry of a number of remarkable evangelists. Included among these were Reginald Radcliffe, Brownlow North, Richard Weaver, Robert Aitken, William Haslam, Duncan Matheson etc. The labors of these men greatly helped to prepare the way for the revival and when the wonderful awakening commenced, they travelled widely across Britain preaching to vast audiences.

The revival in England and Scotland was as definite and striking as the awakening in Ulster. Prayer meetings multiplied in towns and villages and there was a general quickening of spiritual life among Christians. Local revivals were experienced in different places and a great deal of evangelistic work was carried on. Whole congregations were seen bending before the gracious operations of the Holy Spirit like standing corn before a rushing mighty wind.

It is estimated that there were approximately six hundred thousand converts in England and three hundred thousand converts in Scotland as a result of the 1859–60 spiritual awakening.

The Revival in Wales (1859)

The 1859 revival in Wales came in answer to the fervent prayers of burdened Christians. The news of the American revival created in the hearts of many Welsh Christians a "longing" for a spiritual awakening. Many churches held a day of prayer for revival on the first Sunday in August in 1858. In September of that year, Rev. H. Jones returned from America full of the spirit of prayer and revival. The Rev. David Morgan came into contact with him, and soon they were discussing how to set about promoting a revival. They decided that the best way to arouse the country was to organize prayer meetings. Soon the fires of revival began to kindle.

David Morgan, who had received a remarkable enduement of the Spirit, was the most outstanding human instrument during this revival. He visited the countries, towns, and villages, conducting campaigns and preaching in the power of the Holy Spirit. As a result, a tremendous harvest of souls was gathered into the Kingdom.

The population of Wales in 1859 was about one million, and as a direct outcome of the wonderful visitation of the Spirit of God one hundred thousand persons were converted.

The Rev. Evan Jones wrote an account of an extraordinary meeting held on the June 12 and 13. It was typical of many other meetings during the same period.

All appeared to be baptised with the Holy Ghost and fire. Many tears fell and many signs rose up to heaven. This afternoon the cloud burst and the showers fell. The whole house of prayer was a habitation of joy. . . . Heaven was so near. . . . Parents were seen falling on their knees to pray for the children and children for their parents. The earth was thirsting and the heavens pouring. The churches crying, "Come near," and God replying, "I am coming." The seven o'clock meeting came, a heavenly sound was heard in the song of praise, in the reading, and in the prayer. We never heard anything like that. . . .[22]

Revival in Wales (1904)

Forty-five years following the 1859 revival, the fire fell again from heaven upon Wales. As a result of this further gracious outpouring of the Spirit, vast multitudes were saved and spiritual life generally was wonderfully quickened.

During the years immediately prior to the 1904 Welsh revival, there were several local awakenings. The most significant outcome from these developments was the formation of spontaneous prayer meetings, in which all present were free to take part.

At or about this time, Evan Roberts was in college preparing for the ministry. The burden for lost souls came so heavily upon him that he was unable to continue his studies. He said, "Something drew me irresistibly to think of the condition of the lost world."[23] After seeking for some considerable time the baptism of the Holy Spirit, God wonderfully met with him and endued him with power. His life was transformed as a result and he was gripped with a desire to travel throughout Wales with a revival team conducting meetings. He began to pray for a hundred thousand converts and from this time onward talked freely of the revival that was coming to Wales.

God guided him to commence meetings in his home church. The meetings were full of prayer for souls to be saved. During the second week the Spirit of God began to work. Dozens of prayer meetings were being conducted every day throughout the district. Revival was the topic of conversation everywhere and a spirit of great expectancy was abroad.

During the course of the revival which began in Wales, Evan Roberts and his revival party conducted thousands of meetings and tens of thousands of souls were converted. The revival meetings took the form of spontaneous prayer meetings. It was observed that the success of a meeting in saving souls was in proportion to the amount of fervent prayer in that meeting.

In terms of numbers, the Calvinistic Methodists received an added 24,000 into membership; the Wesleyans over 4,000; the Congregationalists 26,500 in 1904–1905. The Anglicans and Baptists brought the total figure to 100,000.[24]

Isle of Lewis Revival (1949)

Due to the growing carelessness towards Sabbath observance and public worship, the spirit of pleasure which had taken hold of the younger generation, the neglect of family worship etc. in the island of Lewis, a number of men and two elderly women entered into a solemn covenant with God to pray until revival came. Together they prayed for many months, pleading the promise, "I will pour water upon him that is thirsty and floods upon the dry ground."[25] In the small hours of a morning, during a remarkable prayer meeting conducted in a barn, a mighty revival began which shook the whole community of Lewis.

The Rev. Duncan Campbell of the Faith Mission was the most prominent evangelist during this revival. His Spirit-anointed ministry was the means of a considerable number of people throughout the island coming to Christ at that time.

> The most remarkable feature of this gracious visitation was not what happened in the Church, but the spiritual impact made upon the island. Men, who until then had no thought of seeking God, were suddenly arrested and became deeply concerned about their soul's salvation.[26]

As a result of the Lewis revival, more began to attend the weekly prayer meeting than attended public worship on the Sabbath before the revival.

There were very few cases of backsliding reported in the years following the Lewis revival. An encouraging number of those converted during the Awakening either went into the Christian ministry or abroad as missionaries to the heathen.

Footnotes

1. W. E. Allen, **The History of Revivals of Religion** (Belfast: Revival Pub. Co., undated), p. 1.
2. James Burns, *Revivals—Their Laws and Leaders* (Grand Rapids, MI: Baker Book House, 1969), p. 163.
3. J. Shearer, *Old Time Revivals* (London: Pickering & Inglis, undated), p. 7.
4. Ibid., p. 10.
5. O. J. Smith, *The Spirit at Work* (London: Marshall, Morgan & Scott, 1946), p. 97.
6. Ibid., p. 105.
7. J. Burns, op. cit., p. 283.
8. Ibid., p. 285.
9. W. E. Allen, op. cit., p. 17.
10. Loc. cit.
11. Ibid., pp. 10–12.
12. *America's Great Revivals,* p. 48.
13. Ibid., p. 75.
14. J. Shearer, op. cit., pp. 82–83.
15. Ibid., p. 81.
16. W. E. Allen, op. cit., pp. 25–26.
17. Ibid., p. 26.
18. W. E. Allen, op. cit., p. 14.
19. W. E. Allen, op. cit., p. 28.
20. J. Shearer, op. cit., p. 93.
21. Ibid., p. 99.
22. W. E. Allen, op. cit., p. 22.
23. W. E. Allen, op. cit., p. 30.
24. E. Evans, *The Welsh Revival of 1904* (London: Evangelical Press, 1969), p. 146.
25. Isaiah 44:3.
26. D. Campbell, *The Price and Power of Revival* (Edinburgh: The Faith Mission Pub., undated), p. 86.

Authors Notes

We repeat here the closing thoughts of the epilogue of this book. We believe that it is theoretically possible to have true revival, even in the closing days of this dispensation. Jesus said: "Lo, I am with you alway, even unto the end of the world" (Matthew 28:20).

But we must first repudiate the false doctrines of decisionism. We must preach sermons which include denunciations of sin and strong Gospel appeals, and pastors must personally counsel those who are awakened by such preaching. We must also cry out strongly to God—pleading with Him to send revival. If we do those things, the way will be clear for God to do the rest, and provide, by His sovereign grace, the missing element of His powerful presence—without which there can be no true revival.

"Call unto me, and I will answer thee, and shew thee great and mighty things, which thou knowest not" (Jeremiah 33:3).

Quotations in this book, from sources other than the Bible, do not imply our full endorsement of everything the person we have quoted has written or said, even in the same book we have cited. We have quoted men favorably who hold various views. We ourselves are independent fundamental Baptists. We hold the historic Baptist position on all essential points. We strongly believe in baptizing the saved, and baptizing them only by immersion. We hold to the autonomy and absolute authority of the local church. We quote only from the KJV, though we reserve the right to refer to the Masoretic Text Hebrew and the Textus Receptus Greek, from which the King James Bible was translated, as did our Baptist forefathers.

This book gives names of those who are in error, as the Bible does. Matthew names Judas and names his sin (Matthew 26:14–16, 47–49); Genesis names Adam and names his sin (Genesis 3:6–19); the Bible gives David's name and his sins (2 Samuel 11:1–12:18); the Bible names Ananias and Sapphira (Acts 5:1–11), Herod (Acts 12:1), Demetrius the silversmith (Acts 19:24–28), Alexander the coppersmith (2 Timothy 4:10), Cain, Balaam, Korah (Jude 11) and many others, in nearly every book of both the Old and New Testaments. We follow the example of God's Word and give the names of those who are in error.

The people or sources mentioned in this book do not necessarily carry the endorsement of Dr. Hymers, Dr. Cagan, or the Fundamentalist Baptist Tabernacle of Los Angeles.

To correspond with Dr. Hymers and Dr. Cagan, write to: The Fundamentalist Baptist Tabernacle, P. O. Box 15308, Los Angeles, California 90015.

Bibliography

Books

Alexander, Archibald. *Sermons of the Log College*. Ligonier, PA: Soli Deo Gloria Publications reprint, 1993.

Alleine, Joseph. *Alarm to the Unconverted* (sometimes titled, *A Sure Guide to Heaven*). Published under the second title by Banner of Truth Trust, Edinburgh, 1959.

Allen, W. E. *The History of Revivals of Religion*. Belfast: Revival Pub. Co. n.d.

Barnes, Albert. *Notes on the New Testament*. Grand Rapids, MI: Baker Book House, 1983, reprinted from the 1885 edition by Blackie & Son, London.

Baxter, Richard. *The Reformed Pastor*. Edinburgh: Banner of Truth Trust, 1989, reprinted from the 1656 edition.

—— *A Treatise on Conversion*. New York: American Tract Society, 1830 edition.

Bellamy, Joseph. *Sin, the Law, and the Glory of the Gospel*. Ames, IA: International Outreach, n.d.

Branson, Roy L. *Church Split*. Bristol, TN: Landmark Publications: 1990.

—— *Dear Abner, I Love You. Joab*. Bristol, TN: Landmark Publications, 1992.

—— *Dear Preacher, Please Quit*. Lancaster, CA: Landmark Publications, 1987.

Bunyan, John. *Pilgrim's Progress*. Material adapted from a simplified version in *Of People*, edited by Ian Anderson. Pensacola,

FL: A Beka Book Publications, 1995.

—— *The Works of John Bunyan.* Edinburgh: Banner of Truth Trust, 1991.

Burgess, Anthony. *Spiritual Refining—The Anatomy of True and False Conversion,* 2 volumes. Ames, IA: International Outreach, n.d.

Burns, James. *Revivals, Their Laws and Leaders.* Grand Rapids, MI: Baker Book House, 1969.

Campbell, Duncan. *The Price and Power of Revival.* Belfast: The Faith Mission, n.d.

Chapell, F. L. *The Great Awakening of 1740.* Philadelphia: American Baptist Publication Society, 1903.

DeHaan, M. R. *The Days of Noah.* Grand Rapids, MI: Zondervan Publishing House, 1963.

Dolan, Jay P. *Catholic Revivalism: The American Experience 1830–1900.* Notre Dame, IN: University of Notre Dame Press, 1978.

Edwards, Brian H. *Revival! A People Saturated With God.* Durham, England: Evangelical Press, 1991.

Edwards, Jonathan. *Sinners in the Hands of an Angry God.* Murfreesboro, TN: Sword of the Lord.

—— *The Works of Jonathan Edwards.* Edinburgh: Banner of Truth Trust, 1992, from the 1834 edition.

Egerton, Gilbert. *Flame of God.* Belfast: Ambassador Publications, 1987.

Evans, E. *The Welsh Revival of 1904.* London: Evangelical Press, 1969.

Finney, Charles G. *An Autobiography.* Old Tappan, NJ: Fleming H. Revell, 1876.

—— *Finney's Systematic Theology.* Minneapolis: Bethany House Publishers, 1994 reprint of 1878 edition.

—— *Lectures on Revivals of Religion.* New York and London: n.p., 1910.

Fuller, David Otis. *Spurgeon's Sermon Notes.* Grand Rapids, MI: Zondervan Publishing House, 1941.

Gerberding, G. H. *The Way of Salvation in the Lutheran Church.*

Philadelphia: Lutheran Publication Society, 1887.

Gerstner, John H. *Jonathan Edwards, Evangelist.* Morgan, PA: Soli Deo Gloria Publications, 1995 reprint.

Gilbert, Martin. *Winston S.Churchill, Volume IV: World in Torment, 1917–1922.* London: William Heinemann, Ltd., 1975.

—— *Winston S. Churchill, Volume V: Prophet of Truth 1922–1939.* London: William Heinemann, Ltd., hardcover edition 1976; Mandarin paperback edition, 1990.

Hayden, Eric W. *Spurgeon on Revival.* Grand Rapids, MI: Zondervan Publishing House, 1962.

Heimert, Alan and Miller, Perry. *The Great Awakening: Documents Illustrating the Crisis and its Consequences.* Old Tappan, NJ: Bobbs-Merrill, 1967.

Hodge, A. A. *The Atonement.* Memphis, TN: Footstool Publications, 1987.

Hodges, Zane. *Grace in Eclipse.* Dallas: Redencion Viva, 1985.

Horton, Michael, editor. *The Agony of Deceit.* Chicago: Moody Press, 1990.

Kroll, Woodrow. *The Vanishing Ministry.* Grand Rapids, MI: Kregel Publications, 1991.

Leupold, H. C. *Exposition of Genesis.* Grand Rapids, MI: Baker BookHouse, 1976.

Lloyd-Jones, David Martyn. *Revival.* Wheaton, IL: Crossway Books,1987.

Luther, Martin. "Preface to the Epistle to the Romans," in *The Works of Martin Luther.* Grand Rapids, MI: Baker Book House, 1982.

MacArthur, John. *The MacArthur Study Bible.* Nashville: Word Publishing, 1997.

Machen, J. Gresham. *Christianity and Liberalism.* Grand Rapids, MI: Wm. B. Eerdmans, reprinted 1983.

Manchester, William. *The Last Lion: Winston Spencer Churchill; Alone 1932–1940.* Boston: Little, Brown, and Company, 1988.

Masters, Peter. *Seven Certain Signs of True Conversion.* London: Sword and Trowel, 1976.

Mattson, J. Stanley. *Charles Grandison Finney and the Emerging Tradition of "New Measure" Revivalism.* Ph.D. dissertation. Chapel Hill, North Carolina: University of North Carolina, 1970.

McGee, J. Vernon. *Thru the Bible,* 5 vols. Nashville: Thomas Nelson, 1983.

McLoughlin, William G., Jr. *Modern Revivalism: Charles Grandison Finney to Billy Graham.* New York: The Ronald Press Company, 1959.

Mead, Matthew. *The Almost Christian.* Morgan, PA: Soli Deo Gloria Publications, 1989.

Morris, Henry M. *The Genesis Record.* Grand Rapids, MI: Baker Book House, 1976.

Murray, Iain H. *David Martyn Lloyd-Jones: The First Forty Years 1899–1939.* Edinburgh: Banner of Truth Trust, 1983.

—— *Revival and Revivalism: the Making and Marring of American Evangelicalism 1750–1858.* Edinburgh: Banner of Truth Trust, 1994.

—— *Spurgeon vs. Hyper-Calvinism.* Edinburgh: Banner of Truth Trust, 1995.

Nettleton, Asahel. *Sermons from the Second Great Awakening.* Ames, IA: International Outreach, 1995 reprint.

—— editor. *Village Hymns for Social Worship.* Ames, IA: International Outreach, n.d.

Nichols, William C. *The Narrow Way.* Ames, IA: International Outreach, 1993.

Packer, J. I. *A Quest for Godliness.* Wheaton, IL: Crossway Books, 1990.

Paisley, Ian R. K. *The Fifty Nine Revival.* Belfast: Martyrs Memorial Free Presbyterian Church, 1987.

Pierson, A. T. *The Bible and Spiritual Life.* New York: Gospel Publishing House, 1908.

Poole, Matthew. *A Commentary on the Holy Bible.* Edinburgh: Banner of Truth Trust, 1990 edition, 3 vols., first edition 1685.

Rabinowitz, Richard. *The Spiritual Self in Everyday Life: The Trans-*

formation of Personal Religious Experience in Nineteenth-Century New England. Boston: Northeastern University Press, 1989.

Reidhead, Paris. *Getting Evangelicals Saved.* Minneapolis, MN: Bethany House Publishers, 1989.

Rice, John R. *Crossing the Deadline.* Murfreesboro, TN: Sword of the Lord.

——— *Hell: What the Bible Says About It.* Murfreesboro, TN: Sword of the Lord.

——— *We Can Have Revival Now!* Murfreesboro, TN: Sword of the Lord, 1950.

——— *What Must I Do To Be Saved?* Murfreesboro, TN: Sword of the Lord, 1945.

——— *Why Preach Against Sin?* Murfreesboro, TN: Sword of the Lord, 1946.

Ryrie, Charles C. *So Great Salvation.* Wheaton, IL: Victor Books, 1989.

Shearer, J. *Old Time Revivals.* London: Pickering & Inglis, n.d.

Smith, O. J. *The Spirit at Work.* London: Marshall, Morgan & Scott, 1946.

Smith, Timothy L. *Revivalism and Social Reform: American Protestantism on the Eve of the Civil War.* New York: Harper, 1965.

Spurgeon, C. H. *Around the Wicket Gate.* Pasadena, TX: Pilgrim Publications, 1992 reprint.

——— *Index* to the *New Park Street Pulpit* and *Metropolitan Tabernacle Pulpit.* Pasadena, TX: Pilgrim Publications.

——— *Lectures to My Students.* Pasadena, TX: Pilgrim Publications, 1990 reprint.

——— *Metropolitan Tabernacle Pulpit*, Pasadena, TX: Pilgrim Publications, 1973 reprint.

——— *New Park Street Pulpit.* Pasadena, TX: Pilgrim Publications, 1981 reprint.

Stoddard, Solomon. *A Guide to Christ.* Ligonier, PA: Soli Deo Gloria Pub., 1993. Reprinted from the 1816 Northampton edition.

Thielicke, Helmut. *Encounter with Spurgeon.* Grand Rapids, MI: Baker Book House, 1975. Includes material quoted from C. H. Spurgeon, "Conversion as Our Aim," in his *Lectures to My Students* New York: Robert Carter & Bros., 1889.

Thiessen, Henry C. *Lectures in Systematic Theology.* Grand Rapids, MI: Wm.B. Eerdmans Publishing Co., 1949.

Toffler, Alvin. *Future Shock.* New York: Bantam Books, 1971.

Tyler, Bennet and Bonar, Andrew. *The Life and Labours of Asahel Nettleton.* Edinburgh: Banner of Truth Trust, 1975; reprinted from the 1854 edition.

Vine, W. E. *An Expository Dictionary of New Testament Words.* Old Tappan, NJ: Fleming H. Revell Co., 1966.

Wells, David F. *Turning to God: Biblical Conversion in the Modern World.* Grand Rapids, MI: Baker Book House, 1989.

Wesley, John. *The Works of John Wesley.* Grand Rapids, MI: Baker Book House, third edition, 1979.

Zodhiates, Spiros. *The Complete Word Study Dictionary of the New Testament.* Chattanooga, TN: AMG Publishers, 1992.

America's Great Revivals. Minneapolis, MN: Bethany House Publishers, no date, no author. Reprinted from *Christian Life* magazine, copyrighted by *Sunday* magazine.

Evangelicals and Catholics Together: The Mission in the Third Millennium. Reprinted by Dr. D. A. Waite, The Bible for Today, Collingswood, New Jersey, no date.

Periodicals

"Born Again Christians Ignorant of Faith," *Baptist Bible Tribune,* April 15, 1996.

Charlesworth, Vernon J. *The Sword and the Trowel,* May, 1876, p. 218.

Horton, Michael S. "The Legacy of Charles Finney," *Modern Reformation* magazine, n.d., posted on computer net April 1, 1996.

Hunt, Dave. *The Berean Call,* April, 1997, p. 3.

Los Angeles *Daily News,* July 2, 1994, p. 19.

Los Angeles *Herald Examiner*, July 14, 1984, p. 24.

Los Angeles *Times*, January 6, 1996, p. B-11.

Los Angeles *Times*, May 3, 1996, p. A-10.

"Metropolitan Tabernacle Statistics," in *The Sword and the Trowel, Volume One: Years 1865, 1866, 1867*. Pasadena, TX: Pilgrim Publications,1995.

National and International Religion Report, October 8, 1990, p. 8.

National and International Religion Report, February 20, 1995, p. 5.

Paisley, Ian R. K. *The Revivalist*. September, 1997.

Pulpit Helps, March, 1996, p. 20.

Rice, John R. *The Sword of the Lord*, printed September 19, 1997.

Spurgeon, C. H. *The Sword and the Trowel*, Volume V, 1877, p. 20. Pasadena, TX: Pilgrim Publications, 1983.

Spurgeon, C. H. *The Sword and the Trowel*, July 1884, p. 439.

"Study: 60 Percent of Adult SBC Baptisms are Rebaptisms," compiled by Baptist Press, in *The California Southern Baptist*, May 4, 1995, p. 8.

The Sword of the Lord, September 19, 1997, p. 24.

What in the World!, published by Bob Jones University, Greenville, South Carolina, volume 19, number 1.

Word, September 20, 1997, p. 19.

Word, October 18, 1997, p. 14.

Other Sources

Hallesby, O. "How Can the Word of God Be Preached So As to Result In Conversion?" from *The Christian Life* by O. Hallesby (Augsburg Publishing House, 1962).

Hayden, Eric W. "Spurgeon's Working Week," from the jacket of volumes 62 and 63 (1916–1917), *Metropolitan Tabernacle Pulpit*. Pasadena, TX: Pilgrim Publications, 1980.

Horton, Michael S. "The Legacy of Charles Finney," from *Modern Reformation* magazine, computer net posting, April 1, 1996.

Hymers, R. L., Jr. "False Conversions—Adapted from 'Sham Conversion' by C. H. Spurgeon," tape recording. Los Angeles: Fundamentalist Baptist Tabernacle.

Rice, John R. "The Price of Revival" (song). Murfreesboro, TN: Sword of the Lord.

Spurgeon, C. H. "Sham Conversion," *Metropolitan Tabernacle Pulpit,* volume 51, pp. 145–56. Pasadena, TX: Pilgrim Publications.

Spurgeon, C. H. "The Warrant of Faith," *Metropolitan Tabernacle Pulpit,* volume 9. Pasadena, TX: Pilgrim Publications, 1979.

Tennent, Gilbert. "The Danger of an Unconverted Ministry," in *Sermons of the Log College,* compiled by Archibald Alexander (Ligonier, PA: Soli Deo Gloria Publications reprint, 1993), pp. 375–404. See also *The Great Awakening: Documents Illustrating the Crisis and Its Consequences* by Alan Heimert and Perry Miller (Old Tappan, NJ: Bobbs-Merrill, 1967), pp. 72–99.

Wilkerson, David. "Who Told You You Are Unworthy?" Times Square Church Pulpit Series, April 4, 1997. Published by World Challenge, Inc., Lindale, Texas, p. 1.

About the Authors

R. L. HYMERS, JR. is a graduate of the California State University at Los Angeles (B.A.), Golden Gate Baptist Theological Seminary, Southern Baptist (M.Div.), San Francisco Theological Seminary, United Presbyterian (D.Min.), and Louisiana Baptist Theological Seminary, Baptist Bible Fellowship (Th.D.). He and his wife, Ileana, are the parents of twin sons, Robert Leslie III and John Wesley. Dr. Hymers worked with Southern Baptist churches for many years. He became a fundamentalist by reading the books and sermons of the late Dr. John R. Rice. Dr. Hymers is the founding pastor of the Fundamentalist Baptist Tabernacle, the only Baptist church in the civic center of Los Angeles. Known for his strong stand for biblical inerrancy and inner-city evangelism, Dr. Hymers is an unashamed old-time fundamentalist, who earnestly contends for the faith in the tradition of J. Frank Norris, John R. Rice, Bob Jones, Sr., and "Fighting Bob" Shuler. He has been in the ministry for over forty years.

CHRISTOPHER CAGAN is a graduate in mathematics from the University of California at Los Angeles (B.A., M.A., Ph.D.). He was a teaching assistant in mathematics at UCLA for several years prior to his conversion. He is also a graduate of Talbot Theological Seminary (M.Div.) and the Claremont Graduate School (M.A., Ph.D.). His second Ph.D. dissertation was written on the subject of apologetics. He is a published expert in the field of stock market analysis, and is currently employed as a statistical analyst. Dr. Cagan's wife, Judith, is a medical doctor. They are the parents of two boys, John Samuel and David. Dr. Cagan is the director of education at the Fundamentalist Baptist Tabernacle. He has been Dr. Hymers' associate for more than twenty years.

RUCKMANISM EXPOSED

by R. L. Hymers, Jr.
M.Div., D.Min., Th.D.

Fundamentalists should read this book. Hymers presents plenty of evidence.

—The Christian News

You will probably read this book straight through. It reveals the connection between the occult, the cults, and the heretical teaching of Ruckanism on the Bible—a demonic doctrine which is shaking the very foundations of fundamentalism at this hour.

Magazine-size book of 67 pages
Contains a bibliography of 61 books.

$5.00

Order from

Dr. R. L. Hymers, Jr.
P.O. Box 15308
Los Angeles, CA 90015